Informing the legislative debate since 1914

Bahrain: Reform, Security, and U.S. Policy

Kenneth Katzman
Specialist in Middle Eastern Affairs

February 14, 2014

Congressional Research Service

7-5700

www.crs.gov

95-1013

Summary

The uprising against Bahrain's Al Khalifa royal family that began in Bahrain on February 14, 2011, amidst other regional uprisings, has not toppled Bahrain's regime or achieved the goals of the mostly Shiite opposition to establish a constitutional monarchy. Demonstrations have continued, although smaller and less frequent since mid-2013, as Bahrain's Shiites seek to bring pressure to bear on the Sunni-dominated government to increase Shiite political influence and rights. The government has arrested and sought to intimidate Shiite leaders while asserting that the opposition is radicalizing, using bombings and other violent tactics against security officials. The crisis has demonstrated that the grievances of the Shiite majority over the distribution of power and economic opportunities were not satisfied by the modest reforms during 1999-2010.

The government and opposition have attempted to resolve the unrest through two "national dialogues" (July 2011 and February – December 2013), but with limited results. A pivotal report by a government-appointed "Independent Commission of Inquiry" (BICI), released November 23, 2011 was critical of the government's actions against the unrest, but outside human rights groups assessed that overall implementation of the 26 BICI recommendations has been modest.

The Obama Administration did not at any time call for an end to the Al Khalifa regime, but it has criticized its use of repressive measures, urged compromise and dialogue, and halted the sale of some arms that the government could potentially use against protesters. The U.S. criticism and arms sales holds have angered some Al Khalifa officials but also dissatisfied the opposition, which asserts that the United States is downplaying regime abuses in order to protect its extensive security relationship with Bahrain. Bahrain has provided key support for U.S. interests by hosting U.S. naval headquarters for the Persian Gulf for over 60 years. The United States signed a formal Defense Cooperation Agreement (DCA) with Bahrain in 1991 and has designated it a "major non-NATO ally." Both these agreements and designations have remained intact through the unrest, and some sales to Bahrain of arms that can only be used for external defense were resumed in May 2012. The United States has continued to expand military facilities in Bahrain—which now accommodate about 7,000 U.S. forces—despite calls by some outside experts to consider relocating U.S. military personnel from Bahrain entirely.

Consumed by its own crisis, Bahrain has joined with but deferred to other GCC powers to resolve political crises in Libya, Syria, and Yemen. Bahrain has strongly criticized the entry of the Iran-backed Shiite group Lebanese Hezbollah into the Syria conflict on the side of President Bashar Al Assad.

Fueling Shiite unrest is the fact that Bahrain is poorer than most of the other Persian Gulf monarchies and therefore lacks ample resources to significantly improve Shiite standards of living. In 2004, the United States and Bahrain signed a free trade agreement (FTA); legislation implementing it was signed January 11, 2006 (P.L. 109-169). The unrest has further strained, although not crippled, Bahrain's economy.

Contents

Figures

Tables

Contacts

The Political Structure, Reform, and Human Rights[1]

The site of the ancient Bronze Age civilization of Dilmun, Bahrain was a trade hub linking Mesopotamia and the Indus valley until a drop in trade from India caused the Dilmun civilization to decline around 2,000 B.C. The inhabitants of Bahrain converted to Islam in the 7th century. Bahrain subsequently fell under the control of Islamic caliphates based in Damascus, then Baghdad, and later Persian, Omani, and Portuguese forces.

The Al Khalifa family, which is Sunni Muslim and generally not as religiously conservative as the leaders of neighboring Saudi Arabia, has ruled Bahrain since 1783. That year, the family, a branch of the Bani Utbah tribe, arrived from the Saudi peninsula and succeeded in capturing a Persian garrison controlling the island. In 1830, the ruling family signed a treaty establishing Bahrain as a protectorate of Britain, which was the dominant power in the Persian Gulf until the early 1970s. As Britain began reducing its responsibilities in the Gulf in 1968, Bahrain and other Persian Gulf emirates (principalities) began deciding on their permanent status. A 1970 U.N. survey (some refer to it as a "referendum") determined that Bahrain's inhabitants preferred independence to Iranian control. Despite that domestic sentiment, in 1971, Bahrain negotiated with other Persian Gulf emirates that ultimately (end of 1971) formed the United Arab Emirates. Difficulties throughout 1971 in reaching agreement on a broad federation caused Bahrain to decide to declare itself independent on August 15, 1971. A U.S. Embassy in Manama, Bahrain's capital, opened in September 1971 in conjunction with Bahrain's independence.

The Ruling Family and Its Dynamics

Bahrain is led by King Hamad bin Isa Al Khalifa (about 61 years old), who succeeded his father, Shaykh Isa bin Sulman Al Khalifa, upon his death in March 1999. Educated at Sandhurst Military Academy in Britain, King Hamad was previously commander of the Bahraini Defense Forces (BDF). The king is considered to be a reformer, but some observers consider him a relatively weak leader unwilling to override hardline, anti-reform Khalifa family members.

The Kings's son, Shaykh Salman bin Hamad, about 44 years old, is Crown Prince. On March 11, 2013, he was appointed first deputy Prime Minister concurrently. Shaykh Salman is U.S.- and U.K.-educated and has long been considered a proponent of accommodation with Bahrain's Shiite majority—about 60% of the approximately 1.25 million person citizenry.[2] Bahrain's Shiite Muslims have long perceived themselves as "second class citizens" who are deprived of a proportionate share of political power and the nation's economic wealth. There are, additionally, an estimated 235,000 expatriates in Bahrain. About 25% of the population is age 14 or younger.

The King's uncle (the brother of the late Amir Isa), Prime Minister Khalifa bin Salman Al Khalifa, has been in position since Bahrain's independence in 1971. He is about 82 years old but

---

[1] Much of the information in this section is from State Department reports: 2012 Country Reports on Human Rights Practices. http://www.state.gov/j/drl/rls/hrrpt/humanrightsreport/index htm#wrapper. CRS has no means to independently investigate the human rights situation in Bahrain or confirm specific allegations of abuses there.

[2] Government officials dispute that the Shiite community is as large a majority as the 70% figure used in most factbooks and academic work on Bahrain. The Shiite community in Bahrain consists of the more numerous "Baharna," who are of Arab ethnicity and descended from Arab tribes who inhabited the area from pre-Islamic times. Shiites of Persian ethnicity, referred to as Ajam, arrived in Bahrain over the past 400 years and are less numerous than the Baharna. The Ajam speak Persian and generally do not integrate with the Baharna or with Sunni Arabs.

believed to be in stable health. He is considered aligned with—although somewhat more politically flexible than—a group of family hard-liners that include Minister of the Royal Court Khalid bin Ahmad bin Salman Al Khalifa[3] and his brother the Commander of the BDF Khalifa bin Ahmad Al Khalifa. The two brothers are known as "Khawalids"—they hail from a branch of the Al Khalifa family that is traced to an ancestor Khalid bin Ali Al Khalifa—and are considered implacably opposed to compromise with the Shiites.[4] The Khawalids reportedly have allies throughout the security and intelligence services and the judiciary. The Royal Court Minister's protégé, Ahmad bin Ateyatallah Al Khalifa (Royal Court minister for "follow-up affairs"), reportedly is an influential hardliner as well. Collectively, the harder liners within and outside the family assert that concessions made to the Shiite majority since 1999 caused the Shiites to increase their political demands rather than satisfied them. In September 2013, Bahrain appointed Lt. Col. Abdullah bin Muhammad bin Rashid, a subordinate of the BDF commander and purported hardliner, to become Ambassador to the United States.

The allies of the Crown Prince within the ruling family—which include a deputy Prime Minister, Muhammad bin Mubarak Al Khalifa (possible successor to the current prime minister)—assert that the level of unrest reached in 2011 would have occurred long ago had the king's reforms not been enacted. The reformists within the family were strengthened by the March 2013 appointment of Crown Prince Salman as first deputy Prime Minister, a new position. The Foreign Minister, Khalid bin Ahmad bin Muhammad Al Khalifa, is a moderate ally of the Crown Prince.[5]

The reforms instituted by King Hamad before the unrest began, although well short of the hopes and expectations the Shiite majority had when he took office, were more extensive than those made by his father, Amir Isa. In December 1992, Amir Isa established a 30-member appointed Consultative Council to comment on proposed laws. In June 1996, he expanded it to 40 members. These reforms did not come close to quieting the demands of either Shiites or Sunnis for the restoration of an elected national assembly, even though Bahrain's Sunnis are considered less hungry for "democracy" than are the Shiites. An elected assembly was provided for under the 1973 constitution but abolished in August 1975 because of fear of sectarian competition and tensions over control of the body. In the years just prior to Shaykh Hamad's accession to rule, there was daily anti-government violence during 1994-1998, mostly by Shiites.

Executive and Legislative Powers

The King, working through the Prime Minister and the cabinet, has broad powers. The King, through the Prime Minister, makes all cabinet appointments. Al Khalifa family members have consistently held about half of all ministerial slots, including all defense, internal security, and foreign policy positions. Before the 2011 unrest, there were only 4 Shiite ministers out of 23 cabinet positions (plus one out of the four deputy prime ministers), and those ministries run by Shiites have been considered less critical. The number of Shiite ministers was increased to six in 2012, in part as a gesture to the opposition. Shiites have also been highly underrepresented in the security forces, serving mainly in administrative tasks. The King appoints all judges by royal decree and he has the authority to amend the constitution.

---

[3] The name of this official is similar to that of the Foreign Minister, Khalid bin Ahmad bin Mohammad Al Khalifa.

[4] Differences between the *khawalids* and others in the family are discussed in, Charles Levinson. "A Palace Rift in Persian Gulf Bedevils Key U.S. Navy Base." Wall Street Journal, February 20, 2013.

[5] The foreign minister's name is similar to, but slightly different from, that of the hardline Royal Court Minister.

As Hamad's first reform steps upon taking office, he assumed the title of King, dropping the more traditional rulership title "Amir," to imply more accountability to the population. He held a referendum on February 14, 2002, that adopted a "National Action Charter," including the text of a constitution. However, many Shiites criticized the constitution because it established that the elected Council of Representatives (COR)[6] and the all-appointed *Shura* (Consultative) Council were of equal size (40 seats each). Together, they constitute a National Assembly (parliament). The government has tended to appoint generally more educated and pro-Western members to the Shura Council, and it is generally more supportive of the government than is the COR, which explains why the opposition seeks maximum authority for the COR. There is no "quota" for females in the National Assembly.

- The Assembly serves as only a partial check on government power, despite constitutional amendments adopted in May 2012 that gave the Assembly greater authority. The amendments declared the elected COR as the presiding chamber of the Assembly, thereby giving it the lead when the two chambers disagree.

- The National Assembly have the power to confirm individual cabinet appointments. However, as a consequence of the May 2012 amendments, it does have the power to reject the government's four-year work plan—and therefore the whole cabinet. The COR has always had the power to remove sitting ministers through a vote of no-confidence (requiring a two-thirds majority). The COR can also, by a similar super-majority, declare that it cannot "cooperate" with the Prime Minister, but the King then rules on whether to dismiss the Prime Minister or disband the COR. None of these actions has ever been taken.

- Either chamber of the National Assembly can originate legislation but enactment into law requires concurrence by the King.[7] Prior to the May 2012 amendments, only the COR could originate legislation. A royal "veto" can be overridden by a two-thirds majority vote of both chambers. A decree issued by the king on August 23, 2012, gives the National Assembly the ability to recommend constitutional amendments, which are then vetted by a "Legislation and Legal Opinion Commission" before consideration by the king.

Political Groups and Elections

Government-opposition disputes over organizing the COR elections predate the 2011 uprising. The Shiite opposition has sought to establish electoral processes that would allow Shiites to translate their numbers into political strength. Elections have been held every four years since 2002, each time marked by substantial tension over perceived government efforts to prevent election of a Shiite majority in the COR. In the COR elections, if no candidate in a contested district wins more than 50% in the first round, a runoff is held one week later.

Formal political parties are banned, but factions organize, for the elections and other political activity, as "political societies"— the functional equivalent of parties:

- *Wifaq*, formally, the Al *Wifaq* (Accord) National Islamic Society, is the largest and most prominent Shiite political society. It is considered a relatively moderate

---

[6] This body is also referred to as the Council of Deputies (Majles al-Nawwab).

[7] Before the May 2012 constitutional amendments, only the COR could draft legislation.

opposition faction and has participated in national dialogue with the government and royal family. A number of Shiite factions are allied with *Wifaq* and have similarly participated in dialogue with the regime; they include the National Democratic Action Society, the National Democratic Assembly, the Democratic Progressive Tribune, and Al Ekhaa. *Wifaq*'s leaders, including overall leader Shaykh Ali al-Salman, have been pressured by the regime. Salman, who is about 45 years old, is a Shiite cleric who has adhered to a tradition in which Bahraini clerics refrain from serving directly in government. He was slightly injured by security forces during a protest in June 2012 and he was arrested on November 3, 2013, and again on December 28, 2013—charged with insulting authorities and "incitement to religious hatred," respectively. His deputy leader, Khalil al-Marzuq, was arrested on September 18, 2013, and charged with "inciting terrorism" for an anti-government speech. Another of *Wifaq*'s top figures, the 75-year-old Shiite cleric Isa Qasim, is considered a hardliner and has resisted many proposals to settle the crisis. His home was raided by the regime in May 2013.

- *Al Haq* (Movement of Freedom and Democracy), another Shiite faction, is outlawed because of its calls for outright change of regime and has boycotted all the COR elections. However, it is smaller in membership than *Wifaq*. Its key leaders are Dr. Abduljalil Alsingace, who is wheelchair-bound, and Hassan Mushaima, both of whom are alleged by the government to have ties to Iran and to Islamist movements in the Middle East. Both have been imprisoned since the February 2011 uprising. Prior to the uprising, Alsingace had visited the United States several times to discuss the human rights situation in Bahrain.

- The Bahrain Islamic Action Society, a small Shiite faction, also is an outlawed faction. It is a successor to the Islamic Front for the Liberation of Bahrain (IFLB), a party purportedly linked Iran-backed extremist actions in Bahrain the 1980s and 1990s. Another IFLB offshoot, Amal, is known as the "Shirazi faction" for its ties to radical Shiite clerics in Iran linked to Ayatollah Shirazi. Amal's leader, Shaykh Muhammad Ali al-Mafoodh, has been in prison since 2011 and Amal was outlawed in 2012.

- *Waad* ("promise") is a left-leaning secular political society whose members are both Sunni and Shiite and is generally aligned with *Wifaq* as an opposition party. Waad's leader, Ibrahim Sharif, has been in prison since 2011.

- Sunni opinion is generally represented by the government. There are some Sunni political societies that support it, but in some cases criticize the government for concessions to the Shiite majority. Two Sunni societies are considered Islamist: *Minbar* (Arabic for "platform"), which is an offshoot of the Muslim Brotherhood, and *Al Asala*, which is a harder-line "Salafist" political society. As noted below, in the 2006-2010 parliament, *Asala* and *Minbar* members held a combined 15 seats. In June 2011, another Sunni grouping formed as a response to the Shiite-led 2011 uprising, organized as a pro-government political society called the National Unity Gathering/National Unity Association. Other Sunni factions that support these groups include Al Saff, the Islamic Shura Society, and the Al Wasat Al Arabi Islamic Society.

Pre-Uprising Elections

Several elections were held during 2002-2010 which suggested to some outside observers that political differences in Bahrain could be resolved electorally and legislatively.

- *2002 Election.* The first elections under the Charter were held in October 2002. In the 2002 election, many Shiite opposition political societies, including *Wifaq*, boycotted the elections on the grounds that setting the COR and the Shura Council at the same size dilutes popular will. The 2002 boycott lowered turnout (about 52%) and helped Sunnis win two-thirds of the 40 COR seats. Of the 170 total candidates, 8 were women, but none of the women was elected.

- *2006 Election: Allegations of Gerrymandering and "Importing Sunnis."* Sunni-Shiite tensions escalated again in advance of the November 25, 2006, parliamentary and municipal elections, aggravated by the Bahraini Shiite perception that a Shiite majority came to power in Iraq through U.S.-backed elections. The election was clouded by allegations, publicly corroborated by a government adviser (Salah al-Bandar) in August 2006, that the government was adjusting election districts to favor Sunni candidates. It was also alleged the government had issued passports to Sunnis in an attempt to shift the demographic balance to the Sunnis' advantage. *Wifaq* and a few other Shiite societies participated, producing a 72% turnout. The Shiite opposition won 17 seats, virtually all those it contested, and became the largest single bloc in the COR, although still short of a majority. Sunni Muslims won 23 total seats, a slight majority. Of those, eight were won by secular Sunnis and 15 by Islamist Sunnis. One woman, who was unopposed in her district, was elected out of 18 female candidates. *Wifaq* boycotted the speakership contest and incumbent COR Speaker Khalifa al-Dhahrani was reelected. The King subsequently named a new Shura Council with 20 Shiites, 19 Sunnis, and one Christian (a female). Ten of the appointees were women. In a nod to the increased Shiite numbers in the COR, the government appointed a Shiite as one of four deputy prime ministers and another, a *Wifaq* supporter, as a minister of state for foreign affairs.

- *The 2010 Elections: Prelude to the Uprising.* The two-round COR vote was held on October 23 and October 30, 2010. Two Bahraini human rights watchdog groups, the Bahrain Human Rights Society and the Bahrain Transparency Society, jointly monitored the elections, along with some international observers. Municipal elections were held concurrently. The electorate was about 300,000 persons, voting in 40 districts spread throughout five governorates. Shiite oppositionists again accused the government of drawing boundaries so as to prevent the election of a Shiite majority. About 200 candidates registered, of whom six were women. Of the six, only Munira Fakhro, a Shiite who was exiled prior to the accession of King Hamad, was endorsed by a political society (*Waad*). *Wifaq* participated despite the arrests of 23 Shiite leaders the previous month under a 2006 anti-terrorism law that gives the government broad powers. The tensions over the 2010 election almost certainly contributed to the major unrest that began in February 2011. espite the pre-election tensions, the election was held without major reports of violence. Turnout was about 67% between the two rounds. The election increased *Wifaq's* representation to 18 seats, although still not a majority; reduced Sunni Islamists to five seats from 15; and empowered by Sunni independents, who won 17 seats, up from nine in the 2006-

2010 parliament. The same one woman won who had won in 2006. In the municipal elections conducted concurrently, one woman was elected in the second round—the first woman to be elected to a municipal council.

In advance of the December 14, 2010, start of the parliamentary term, the King reappointed 30 of the 40 serving Shura Council members and ten new members. Of its membership, 19 were Shiites, including the speaker, Ali bin Salih al-Salih. The Council has four women, substantially fewer than the 2006-2010 Council that had nine. Among the four, one is Jewish (Nancy Khadouri), out of a Jewish population in Bahrain of about 40 persons, and one is Christian (Hala Qarrisah). Bahrain has an estimated 1,000 Christians.

Table 1. Comparative Composition of National Assembly

	2006	2010	Post-By-Election (October 2011)
Council of Representatives (COR)			
Wifaq (Shiite Islamist)	17	18	0
Shiite Independent	0	0	8
Sunni Independent (mostly secular) in COR	8	17	27
Moderate Sunni Islamist (Minbar, Muslim Brotherhood)	7	2	2
Conservative Sunni Islamist (Asala, Salafi)	8	3	3
COR Sect Composition	23 Sunni, 17 Shiite	22 Sunni, 18 Shiite	32 Sunni, 8 Shiite
Women in COR	1	1	4
Shura Council (Upper House, appointed)			
Sectarian, Religious Composition Upper House (Shura Council)	20 Shiite, 19 Sunni, 1 Christian	19 Shiite, 19 Sunni, 1 Christian, 1 Jew	Same as before
Number of Women	9	4	same

2011 Uprising: Origin, Developments, and Prognosis

King Hamad's efforts to satisfy Shiite aspirations were demonstrated to have failed when a major uprising began on February 14, 2011, in the aftermath of the uprising that toppled Egypt's President Hosni Mubarak.[8] After a few days of protests and minor confrontations with security forces, mostly Shiite demonstrators converged on the interior of a major traffic circle, "Pearl Roundabout," named after a statue there depicting Bahrain's pearl-diving past. The protesters

---

[8] The events of the uprising, and the government's political and security reaction, are examined in substantial detail in the Bahrain Independent Commission of Inquiry (BICI) report released November 23, 2011. Text of the report is at http://files.bici.org.bh/BICIreportEN.pdf.

demanded altering the constitution to expand the powers of the COR; ending gerrymandering of election districts to favor Sunnis; providing more jobs and economic opportunities; and replacing hard-line Prime Minister Khalifa. On February 15, 2011, King Hamad formed a committee to investigate the use of force against protestors, which killed two by that time.

The unrest took on new dimensions in the early morning of February 17, 2011, when security forces surrounded the thousands of demonstrators in Pearl Roundabout and used rubber bullets and tear gas to remove them from the location. Four demonstrators were killed. Additional protests took place on February 18, 2011, with several protesters shot. *Wifaq* pulled all 18 deputies out of the COR, and Britain closed its embassy and banned arms exports to Bahrain. In part at the reported urging of the United States, on February 19, 2011, the government pulled security forces back, and demonstrators reentered the Roundabout. On February 22 and 25, 2011, demonstrations said to be perhaps the largest in Bahrain's history were held. These followed a large demonstration on February 21, 2011, by government supporters. (Wifaq and other Shiite groups boycotted a September – October 2011 special election to fill those seats, producing a COR with 32 Sunni to only 8 Shiite-held seats.)

The government, with Crown Prince Salman leading the effort, invited the representatives of the protesters to begin a formal dialogue. That effort was supported by a gesture by King Hamad on February 22, 2011, to release or pardon 308 Bahrainis, including *Al Haq* leader Mushaima, paving the way for him to return from exile. On February 26, 2011, the King dropped two Al Khalifa family members from cabinet posts as a gesture to the opposition.

Crown Prince Salman's "Seven Principles" Reform Plan

On March 13, 2011, Crown Prince Salman articulated "seven principles" that would guide a national dialogue, including a "parliament with full authority"; a "government that meets the will of the people"; fair voting districts; and several other measures.[9] The articulation of the seven principles gave *Wifaq* and other moderate oppositionists hope that many of their demands could be met through dialogue. However, anger at the government's use of force appeared to shift many demonstrators closer to hardline groups such as *Al Haq* that demanded an end to the monarchy.[10]

The Saudi-led Intervention

With Shiite groups refusing to accept the offer of dialogue, protests escalated and sparked broader Sunni-Shiite clashes. On March 13, 2011, despite the Crown Prince's articulation of his "seven points," protesters blockaded the financial district of the capital, Manama, prompting governmental fears that the unrest could choke this major economic sector. Bahrain requested that the Gulf Cooperation Council (GCC), of which it is a member, send security forces to protect key sites and, on March 14, 2011, a GCC force (from the GCC joint Peninsula Shield unit) spearheaded by a reported 1,200 Saudi armored forces and 600 UAE police crossed into Bahrain and took up positions at key locations. Kuwait sent naval forces to help Bahrain secure its maritime borders. On March 15, 2011, King Hamad declared (Royal Decree Number 18) a three-month state of emergency. Bahrain's security forces, freed up by the GCC deployment, cleared

---

[9] BICI report, op. cit., p. 165.

[10] "Bahrain Hard-Liners Call for Royal Family to Go." Cable News Network website, March 9, 2011.

demonstrators from Pearl Roundabout and demolished the Pearl Monument on March 18, 2011.[11] That action caused remaining Shiite ministers in the cabinet, many of the Shiites in the Shura Council, and many Shiites in other senior posts, to suspend their work or resign. Most public protests in downtown Manama ceased.

Perceiving the regime had gained the upper hand, the King announced in May 2011 that the state of emergency would end on June 1, 2011, two weeks earlier than scheduled. The government held to the new schedule and the GCC forces began to depart in late June 2011. King Hamad spoke to the population on May 31, 2011, to mark the end of the emergency, offering unconditional dialogue with the opposition beginning July 1, 2011. The GCC armed intervention represented an escalation from earlier steps to help the Bahrain government. The GCC states had earlier about $20 billion to help both Bahrain (and Oman, which also faced unrest) by fueling job creation. In April 2013, Kuwait continued the effort by pledging an additional $1.3 billion for development projects in Bahrain.

"National Dialogue" Begun and Inquiry Commission Established

On June 29, 2011, as a further gesture toward the opposition, the king named a five-person "Bahrain Independent Commission of Inquiry," (BICI) headed by highly regarded international legal expert Dr. Cherif Bassiouni, to investigate the government's response to the unrest that began in February. It held a public forum on July 24, 2011, but came under criticism from Shiite opposition figures who interpreted certain Bassiouni statements as exonerating top officials.

The naming of the BICI set the stage for the "National Dialogue" on political and economic reform to begin on July 2, 2011, under the chairmanship of speaker of the COR Dhahrani. About 300 delegates participated, of which the Shiite opposition broadly comprised 40-50 delegates, of which 5 belonged to *Wifaq*.[12] Over several weeks, the dialogue addressed political, economic, social, and human rights issues that senior Bahraini officials said was intended to outline a vision of Bahrain rather than specific steps. The detention of many oppositionists hung over the meetings, and *Wifaq* exited the talks on July 18, 2011. Others noted that the Crown Prince did not chair the meetings, suggesting he was eclipsed by hard line figures within the royal family.

The dialogue concluded in late July 2011 after reaching consensus on the following recommendations, which were endorsed by the government on July 29, 2011.

- an elected parliament (lower house) with expanded powers, including the power to confirm or reject a nominated cabinet; the power to confirm or veto the government's four-year work plan; the right to discuss any agenda item; and the power for the full COR to question ministers on their performance or plans. In addition, the overall chairmanship of the National Assembly should be exercised by the elected COR, not the Shura Council.

- a government "reflecting the will of the people."

- "fairly" demarcated electoral boundaries.

---

[11] Some accounts differ on the involvement of the Peninsula Shield force, with some observers arguing that members of the force participated directly in suppressing protests, and others accepting the Bahrain/GCC view that the GCC force guarded key locations and infrastructure.

[12] Mohamed Hasni. "Bahrain Opens Dialogue Buoyed by Shiite Attendance." Agence France Presse, July 2, 2011.

- reworking of laws on naturalization and citizenship.

- combating financial and administrative corruption.

- efforts to reduce sectarian divisions.

There were reportedly 82 economic recommendations, including new mechanisms to provide food subsidies to only the most needy citizens.

As a gesture of reconciliation after the dialogue concluded, in a speech on August 28, 2011, near the conclusion of the holy month of Ramadan, King Hamad announced the pardoning of some protesters and the reinstatement of some of the approximately 2,700 of those who had been fired for alleged participation in unrest. On August 8, 2011, the government released the two jailed *Wifaq* COR deputies, Matar and Fairuz, along with several other activists.

"Manama Document:" Opposition Counter-Proposal. Wifaq and other Shiite opposition groups rejected the outcome of the national dialogue as failing to fulfill even the Crown Prince's offer of a parliament with "full authority." The groups, led by *Wifaq* and *Waad,* unveiled their own proposals – the "Manama Document" - on October 12, 2011. The manifesto called for a fully elected one-chamber parliament with legislative powers, the direct selection of the prime minister by the largest coalition in the elected legislature, and the running of elections by an independent election commission. The opposition also viewed the government's pledge of "fairly demarcated" election boundaries as vague, and likely to enable the government to continue to gerrymander districts to ensure a Sunni majority in the lower house.

Dialogue Recommendations Produce Constitutional Amendments

Despite the opposition's criticism of the dialogue results, the government appointed a committee, headed by deputy Prime Minister Muhammad Mubarak Al Khalifa, to implement the consensus recommendations. After rounds of meetings between both houses of the National Assembly and various ministries, the government drafted amendments to the Bahraini constitution. They were announced by the King on January 16, 2012, adopted by the National Assembly, and ratified by the King on May 3, 2012. The amendments:

- Imposed limitations on the power of the king to appoint the members of the Shura Council, and a requirement that he consult the heads of the two chambers of the National Assembly before dissolving the COR.

- Gave either chamber of the National Assembly the ability to draft legislation or constitutional amendments.

- Changed the overall chair of the National Assembly to the speaker of the elected COR instead of the chairman of the appointed Shura Council.

- Gave the COR the ability to veto the government's four-year work plan— essentially an ability to veto the nomination of the entire cabinet—without the concurrence of the Shura Council. This was an expansion of previous powers to vote no confidence against individual ministers.

The BICI Report and Implementation Process

In addition to the national dialogue, the government looked to the release of the BICI report to help resolve the crisis. The focus of the BICI mission was how the government handled the unrest—and not on competing ideas for political reform. It was initially due by October 30, 2011, but was released on November 23, 2011. The 500+ page report provided some support for the narratives of both sides in the crisis, and recommendations, including[13]

- There was "systematic" and "deliberate" use of excessive force, including torture and forced confessions, against protesters.

- The opposition articulated additional demands as the uprising progressed.

- The government did not provide evidence to establish a link between the unrest in Bahrain and the government of Iran. (p. 378)

- There was no evidence of human rights abuses committed by the GCC forces that intervened at the request of the Bahraini government. (p. 378)

The report contained 26 recommendations (pp. 411-415) to try to prevent future violence against peaceful protesters and to hold accountable those responsible for abuses against protesters. In keeping with the BICI's mandate, the recommendations did not address the political structure of Bahrain. Apparently recognizing that it would be judged by the international community on its response to the report, King Hamad issued a statement accepting the criticism and promising full implementation of the recommendations. *Wifaq* supported the parts of the report that support its accounts but criticized it as failing to state that abuse of protesters were deliberate government policy. On November 26, 2011, King Hamad issued a royal order to establish a 19-member National Commission to oversee implementation of the recommendations, chaired by Shura Council Chairman Ali al-Salih (a Shiite). The King also announced that the "National Human Rights Institution," established in 2010, would be fully independent of the government.

On March 20, 2012, the National Commission issued its final report, generally supporting the government's assertions of its implementation steps to that date.[14] In the cover letter to its report, the National Commission stated that "the reader will see that in less than 100 days this Commission has worked hard with the Government to reform the justice, human rights, policing, security services and media sectors in a way that accords with best international practice."

Subsequently, a "Follow-Up Unit," headed by Ms. Dana Al Zayani, was established by the Ministry of Justice.[15] According to the government, the National Commission, and the Follow Up Unit, the government implemented the vast majority of the 26 BICI recommendations. However, a study by the Project on Middle East Democracy (POMED), issued on the one-year anniversary of the BICI recommendations, found that the government had fully implemented only three of the recommendations, partially implemented 15, not implemented six at all, and two others had "unclear" implementation.[16] This more critical assessment was supported by BICI chair Bassiouni in public comments marking the one-year anniversary of the report. The conference report on the FY2013 defense authorization act, H.R. 4310 (P.L. 112-239, signed January 2, 2013) directed the

---

[13] http://files.bici.org.bh/BICIreportEN.pdf.

[14] The full text of the National Commission's March 20, 2012, report is at http://www.biciactions.bh/wps/portal/BICI/.

[15] The Follow-Up Unit's June report can be found at http://www.iaa.bh/downloads/bici_followup_report_en.pdf.

[16] POMED. "One Year Later: Assessing Bahrain's Implementation of the BICI Report." November 2012.

Secretary of State to report to Congress within 180 days of enactment (by July 2, 2013) on Bahrain's implementation of the BICI recommendations. (A formal provision of the law to this effect was taken out in conference and substituted with conference report language to the same effect.) The report was submitted but not made public;[17] press reports indicate that it concluded that the government had fully implemented five out of the 26 recommendations—a finding broadly similar to those of POMED and other outside groups.[18]

The recommendations that observers agree were fully implemented include

- Stripping the National Security Agency of law enforcement powers and limiting it to purely intelligence gathering. That occurred with the issuing of an amendment to the 2002 decree establishing that agency. The head of the organization was removed and replaced by Adel bin Khalifa Al Fadhil, a non-royal.

- Drafting and providing training on a code of conduct for the police, based on international best practices. The government hired former Miami police chief John Timoney and former British police chief John Yates to teach Bahraini police tactics and techniques that conform to international standards of human rights practices. However, the State Department's human rights report for 2012, issued on April 19, 2013, says that the Ministry of Interior's enforcement of the code of conduct is unclear.[19]

- Training judiciary employees and prosecutors on preventing and eradicating torture and ill-treatment.

There appears to be broad agreement among observers, including the State Department, human rights groups, Bassiouni, and others, that the government has not implemented several recommendations (5, 8, 10, 14, 22, and 24) that address investigation and prevention of torture, detention without prompt access to legal counsel, dropping charges on those who protested but did not use violence, and allowing the opposition free expression and access to media.

Most of the recommendations fall into an intermediate category of partial implementation:

- Holding security officials accountable for abuses (recommendations No. 2 and No. 7). There appears to be agreement that the government has shielded high-ranking officials from prosecution while allowing prosecution of lower-ranking officers. In September 2012, seven police lieutenants were referred to criminal courts for alleged mistreatment and torture allegations against medical staff detained during the unrest.

- Referral of all cases of security personnel who committed major abuses to the public prosecutor for subsequent prosecution. On March 13, 2013, two police officers were sentenced to 10 years in prison for fatally beating protesters in 2011. In July 2013, the government appointed Nawaf al-Maawdah as the police ombudsman to examine cases filed against security personnel for causing death or physical harm.

---

[17] Author conversation with congressional staff, July 2013.

[18] http://mideast.foreignpolicy.com/posts/2013/10/14/the_peril_of_ignoring_bahrain_s_iron_fist.

[19] http://www.state.gov/j/drl/rls/hrrpt/humanrightsreport/index htm#wrapper. p.11.

- Abolition of the military court system and transfer of all cases to ordinary courts.

- Establishment of new procedures to record interrogations of detainees (No. 13).

- Integrating Shiites into the security services (No. 11). On September 17, 2012, the government announced hiring of 500 police cadets "representing all communities in Bahrain"—in an effort to address this recommendation.

- Reinstatement of fired workers, public sector employees, and students (No. 18, No. 19, and No. 20). Almost all of the over 2,500 dismissed workers have been reinstated.

- Establishment of a compensation fund for the victims of torture and families of deceased victims (No.16 and No. 17). In August 2011, the King announced the "Civil Settlement Initiative" fund setting aside over $25 million to compensate these victims.

- The rebuilding of destroyed religious sites (No. 21). At least five of the more than 53 Shiite religious sites demolished by the regime during the course of the uprising have been mostly rebuilt. Rebuilding of another 17 sites is in various stages of construction.

Second National Dialogue

Continued demonstrations, use of force against them, and increasing incidents of anti-government violence caused the government and the opposition to seek to resume dialogue. Moderates on both sides stressed that the Crown Prince's "Seven Principles," the national dialogue consensus recommendations, and the Manama Document had many points in common. The U.S. State Department sought to foster momentum for resumed dialogue by promoting "Track 2" meetings that might examine ideas for a compromise. A British national, Jonathan Powell, formerly chief of staff to then-Prime Minister Tony Blair, reportedly provided *Wifaq* activists with reconciliation training. The Bahraini government rejected a U.S. idea to tap name a high-level international mediator to narrow the differences between the parties.

Momentum for renewed dialogue appeared in late 2012. The State Department praised the Crown Prince's speech at the December 7-8, 2012, Manama Dialogue (annual international security conference sponsored by the International Institute for Strategic Studies) calling for a resumption of national dialogue. On January 22, 2013, the King formally reiterated his earlier calls for a restart of the dialogue and, the same day, *Wifaq* and five allied parties (Waad, the National Democratic Gathering Society, the Unitary National Democratic Assemblage, the Democratic Progressive Tribune, and the Ekhaa National Society) accepted the invitation.

The new dialogue began on February 10, 2013, consisting of twice per week meetings attended by: the Minister of Justice (an Al Khalifa family member) and two other ministers, eight opposition representatives (*Wifaq* and allied parties), eight representatives of pro-government organizations, and five members of the National Assembly (both the upper and lower house). To facilitate progress, the King appointed Crown Prince Salman first deputy Prime Minister (March 11, 2013).

The second national dialogue quickly bogged down and produced few results. The opposition insisted any consensus recommendations be put to a popular referendum, while the government and its allies insisted that agreements be enacted by the National Assembly. The opposition demanded that the dialogue include authoritative decision makers and representatives of the King—higher-level figures than the ministers that were participating. The opposition participants began boycotting the talks in mid-September 2013, to protest lack of progress as well as the arrest of Khalil al-Marzuq, the deputy chief of *Wifaq* and *Wifaq*'s representative to the dialogue. The government formally suspended the dialogue on January 8, 2014.

In an unexpected development, Crown Prince Salman sought to revive the dialogue process by meeting with Marzuq and overall *Wifaq's* leader Shaykh Salman on January 15, 2014. The Crown Prince convened the meeting despite the fact that both faced criminal charges in separate cases. The meeting appeared to address the main *Wifaq* demand that political dialogue be conducted with senior Al Khalifa members. A travel ban on Shaykh Salma related to charges against him was lifted subsequent to that meeting. Still, suggesting continuing divisions in the regime, the harder line Minister of the Royal Court Shaykh Khalid bin Ahmad Al Khalifa (see above) subsequently met with opposition representatives and asked them to present proposals for altering Bahrain's governing structure. The Minister's office subsequently stated it would review these ideas before convening a new iteration of the national dialogue process.

Prospects for Dialogue and the Uprising

Some experts express optimism that dialogue will eventually produce a settlement. *Wifaq* leader Shaykh Salman has offered as an interim compromise the formation of a "national unity government" in which the opposition gains half the seats in a new cabinet. In the course of the second national dialogue, the government and the opposition discussed negotiations on "power sharing"—the possibility of bringing the opposition into the cabinet. And, some senior Saudi officials have met with Bahraini opposition figures—a sign of possible softening of the Saudi position that has been against any Bahraini government compromise with the opposition. Earlier, a widely discussed interim compromise was the replacement of Prime Minister Khalifa, who is widely despised by the opposition, with a moderate opposition figure. Some oppositionists have said they would even accept a Sunni, but not a member of the royal family, as a replacement for the current prime minister. The government did not agree to this step even though, throughout the crisis, some Bahrain government supporters appeared to be sympathetic to it.[20]

Others are pessimistic about the prospects for a solution because demonstrations have continued, although of greater frequency and intensity in the Shiite villages ringing Manama rather than the downtown area. The opposition called three days of demonstrations (February 14-16, 2014) to mark the third anniversary of the uprising, and 29 persons were arrested as they tried to converge on central Manama on February 14, 2014. Continued abuses by Bahraini security forces—including use of tear gas against demonstrators and raids on homes of suspected dissidents and protesters—suggest that the main goal of the BICI process was not accomplished. And, as noted above, the government has become somewhat more aggressive in arresting and prosecuting leaders of *Wifaq* and other opposition factions.

Emerging Insurgency? Others are pessimistic on the basis that the uprising shows potential to evolve into a violent insurgency. One relatively new hardline group, the "14 February Coalition" (anniversary of the Bahrain uprising) claims to be inspired by the "Tamarod" (rebel)-led protests in Egypt that prompted the Egyptian military to remove Muslim Brotherhood president Mohammad Morsi. The government asserts that the 14 February Coalition is a terrorist movement

---

[20] Author conversations with representatives of and observers close to the regime. April 2011.

that seeks to overthrow the state, and the movement gave some support to that assertion when it claimed responsibility for an April 14, 2013, explosion in the Financial Harbour district. On September 29, 2013, 50 Shiites were sentenced to up to 15 years in prison for alleged involvement in the 14 February Coalition.

Other acts or intended acts of violence have been conducted by unspecified groups or persons. On April 9, 2012, an improvised explosive device killed seven police. In apparent retaliation, Sunni citizens ransacked a supermarket owned by a Shiite business group (Jawad Group) the following day. On June 14, 2012, the government discovered bomb-making materials in several locations. On November 5, 2012, two non-Bahrainis were killed in five explosions from homemade bombs. Several police officers were wounded by a roadside bomb on January 31, 2013. On April 29, 2013, the government claimed to have uncovered an arms warehouse used by oppositionists. On May 30, 2013, and July 14, 2013, home-made bombs wounded a total of 11 police officers. On October 7, 2013, a Bahrain court convicted nine Bahraini Shiites linked to the bomb-making facilities discussed above for "forming a militant group" and making explosives for attacks to destabilize the Kingdom. On December 28, 2013, two police officers were severely wounded by a bombing on the outskirts of Manama. On December 30, 2013, following a two-day raid, authorities seized a ship, originating in Iraq, allegedly carrying Iranian weaponry and bomb-making material for the Bahrain opposition.[21]

Wifaq and other mainstream opposition groups have denounced any use of violence, while at the same time accusing the government of exaggerating the incidents discussed above. Pro-government Bahrainis say that the increasing instances of violence and bombings shows intent of the opposition to overthrow the regime by any means necessary. Should the uprising evolve into a violent uprising, the ascension of a Shiite-led regime is possible, although the GCC determination to prevent this makes this outcome unlikely.

Table 2. Status of Prominent Dissidents/Other Metrics of the Uprising

Abdul Hadi al-Khawaja, founder of Bahrain Center for Human Rights	Arrested April 9, 2011, was one of 13 prominent dissidents tried by state security court May 8, 2011, and sentenced to life in prison for conspiring to overthrow the government and for espionage on June 22, 2011. He conducted a hunger strike in prison in early 2012 but was force fed by Bahraini officials and remains alive. Daughters Zainab and Maryam have been repeatedly arrested for opposition activities, and have campaigned abroad for their father's release and for the Shiite opposition generally. His brother, Salah Abdullah al-Khawaja, was sentenced that day to five years in prison. Both sentences upheld September 4, 2012.
Hassan Mushaima and Dr. Abduljalil Alsingace, Al Haq leaders	Two of the 13 prominent dissidents tried by state security court May 8, 2011, sentenced to life in prison on June 22, 2011. Sentence upheld September 4, 2012. Mushaima's son was one of the 31 whose citizenship was revoked in November 2012.
Other prominent oppositionists sentenced on June 22, 2011	Along with the Khawaja brothers, Mushaima, and Alsingace, the June 22, 2011, sentences of nine other prominent dissidents were upheld on September 4, 2012, and reaffirmed by the Court of Cassation on January 8, 2013. Of the nine, four are sentenced to life in prison—Abdulwahab Ahmed; Mohammad al-Saffaf; Abduljalil Mansour; and Said Mirza Ahmad. State Department said on September 4, 2012, it was "deeply troubled" by the upholding of the sentences.
Nabeel Rajab	Successor to al-Khawaja as head of BCHR. Arrested February 15, 2012, for inciting illegal assembly and organizing unlicensed demonstrations, released, and rearrested on April 1, 2012. Sentenced on August 16, 2012, to three years in jail but, on December 11, 2012,

---

[21] Sandeep Singh Grewal. Arms Ring is Smashed by Police. Daily News, December 31. 2013.

	sentence was reduced to two years on appeal.
Mohammad al Maskati	President of the Bahrain Youth Society for Human Rights, arrested October 16, 2012, for taking part in illegal gatherings. Released the following day.
Sayed Yousif al-Muhafdha	Member of the Bahrain Center for Human Rights, has catalogued and reported on protests over social media. Arrested December 17, 2012, and detained for two weeks in November 2012.
21 medical personnel from Salmaniya Medical Complex	Twenty-one medical personnel were arrested in April 2011 and subsequently tried for inciting sectarian hatred, possession of illegal weapons, and forcibly occupying a public building. The personnel argued that they were helping wounded protesters. They were tried in a military court before the government announced their retrial in a civilian court. All were eventually acquitted, most recently in late March 2013 by an appeals court. However, they have not been able to regain their jobs at the medical center. In December 2013, two police officers were cleared of torturing the medics to obtain confessions.
Matar Matar and Jawad Fairuz, members of the COR, Ayatollah Najati	Arrested May 2, 2011, and released August 8, 2011. Matar formally acquitted on February 19, 2012. Fairuz was one of the 31 whose citizenship was revoked in Nov. 2012. His brother, Jalal Fairuz, was another stripped of citizenship, as was Shiite Ayatollah Hussein al-Najati.
Number killed in the uprising to date	About 90

Sources: Various press and interest group reports.

U.S. Posture on the Uprising

The Administration has not at any time called for the Al Khalifa regime to step down, asserting that Bahrain's use of force against demonstrators has been limited and that the Bahrain government has—prior to and since the uprising began—undertaken reform. The Administration has repeatedly urged Bahraini authorities against using force against protesters, it opposed the GCC intervention, and it has called on all parties to engage in sustained political dialogue on reforms.[22] After the GCC intervention, on March 19, 2011, then Secretary Clinton said:

> Bahrain obviously has the sovereign right to invited GCC forces into its territory under its defense and security agreements.... [The United States has] made clear that security alone cannot resolve the challenges facing Bahrain. As I said earlier this week, violence is not and cannot be the answer. A political process is. We have raised our concerns about the current measures directly with Bahraini officials and will continue to do so.

President Obama's May 19, 2011, speech on the uprisings in the Middle East said the prospects for success of a Bahrain government dialogue with the opposition were compromised by the jailing of opposition figures. This position was restated in separate June 7, 2011, meetings between the Crown Prince and then Secretary Clinton and President Obama. In his September 21, 2011, speech to the U.N. General Assembly, President Obama said:

> In Bahrain, steps have been taken toward reform and accountability. We're pleased with that, but more is required. America is a close friend of Bahrain, and we will continue to call on the government and the main opposition bloc—the *Wifaq*—to pursue a meaningful dialogue that brings peaceful change that is responsive to the people. We believe the patriotism that binds

---

[22] Secretary of State Clinton Comments on the Situation in the Middle East. http://www.youtube.com/watch?v=GbucMZUg3Gc.

Bahrainis together must be more powerful than the sectarian forces that would tear them apart. It will be hard, but it is possible.

The same day, Ambassador-nominee to Bahrain Thomas Krajeski testified in confirmation hearings before the Senate Foreign Relations Committee, saying the government "overreacted" to the unrest. He also praised the government's record of reform. (He was confirmed as Ambassador to Bahrain.)

After the release of the BICI report,then Secretary of State Clinton said that the United States is

> deeply concerned about the abuses identified in the report ... and believe[s] that the BICI report offers a historic opportunity for all Bahrainis to participate in a healing process that will address long-standing grievances and move the nation onto a path of genuine, sustained, reform.

During May 2012, Crown Prince Salman visited Washington, DC, and met with Secretary of State Clinton, Secretary of Defense Panetta, and Vice President Biden. As discussed below, a resumption of some U.S. arms sales to Bahrain was announced on May 11, 2012, which represented an Administration effort to strengthen the reformist Crown Prince politically.

Among recent statements, on June 6, 2013, Secretary of State John Kerry met in Washington, D.C., with the Crown Prince and a subsequent State Department statement said: the United States and Bahrain "agreed that all sides should contribute constructively to reconciliation, meaningful dialogue, and reform that meets the aspirations of all Bahrainis. Secretary Kerry reiterated [the U.S.] belief that all sides must reject violence and pursue actions that will contribute to Bahrain's future growth and prosperity." Secretary of Defense Chuck Hagel visited Bahrain to speak before the 2013 Manama Dialogue (IISS security conference discussed above), becoming the first U.S. cabinet member to visit Bahrain since the 2011 uprising began. Subsequently, in late January 2014, acting Assistant Secretary of State for Democracy, Human Rights, and Labor Uzra Zeya visited Bahrain to meet with senior officials there.

Although the Obama Administration has continued military and anti-terrorism assistance and some arms sales to Bahrain, some U.S. aid and sales are on hold or are at reduced levels from what was expected before the unrest began. For example, $25 million in military aid (Foreign Military Financing, FMF) was requested for Bahrain for FY2012 (figures determined just before the uprising began), but only $10 million was provided, and the same $10 million was and is being provided in FY2013 and in FY2014. The Administration has not imposed any sanctions on Bahrain or on Bahraini officials for human rights abuses.

Critics of the Administration—primarily human rights-oriented groups such as Human Rights Watch and the Project on Middle East Democracy[23]—say the U.S. response has been colored by the vital U.S. security interests in Bahrain rather than a commitment to promoting human rights. Critics add that the Administration is concerned, excessively so in the view of these critics, that a fall of the Al Khalifa regime and ascension of a Shiite-led government could increase Iran's influence and lead to an unwanted loss of the U.S. use of Bahrain's military facilities. Administration critics have said that continued military sales and aid to the government represents a tacit endorsement of the government's stance on the unrest. Some outside experts criticized State Department spokeswoman Marie Harf's September 18, 2013, reaction to the arrest

---

[23] Stephen McInerny. "Silence on Bahrain." *Washington Post* op-ed. November 5, 2012.

of Khalil al-Marzuq because her comments expressed disappointment not at the arrest but at the opposition's pullout from the national dialogue. She amended those comments the following day in a statement criticizing the government's decrees placing limits on peaceful assembly.

Some human rights-related groups have suggested that the United States should ban travel to the United States or freeze any U.S.-based assets of Bahraini officials determined by the Administration to have committed or authorized human rights abuses against peaceful protesters. Such sanctions have been imposed on members of adversary governments such as Syria and Iran, for example in the Comprehensive Iran Sanctions, Accountability, and Divestment Act of 2012 (P.L. 111-195).

Pre-2011 U.S. Posture on Bahraini Democracy and Human Rights

Well before the 2011 unrest began, human rights groups and Bahraini Shiite oppositionists had accused successive U.S. Administrations of downplaying government abuses. Critics point to then Secretary of State Clinton's comments in Bahrain on December 3, 2010, referring to the October 2010 elections, saying: "I am impressed by the commitment that the government has to the democratic path that Bahrain is walking on. It takes time; we know that from our own experience."[24]

The Administration counters the criticism with assertions that, for many years prior to the 2011 unrest, the United States sought to accelerate political reform in Bahrain and to empower its political societies through several programs. The primary vehicle has been the "Middle East Partnership Initiative (MEPI)," which began funding programs in Bahrain in 2003. MEPI funds have been used to help Bahrain build an independent judiciary, to strengthen the COR, to empower women, to conduct media training, and to promote legal reform. MEPI funds have also been used to fund AFL-CIO projects with Bahraini labor organizations, and to help Bahrain implement the U.S.-Bahrain FTA. In May 2006 Bahrain revoked the visa for the resident program director of the National Democratic Institute (NDI), and did not allow the office to reopen. NDI was conducting programs to enhance parliamentary capabilities through a local NGO. In February 2010, the MEPI office of State Department signed a memorandum of understanding with Bahrain to promote entrepreneurship there and promote opportunities for trade with U.S. small businesses. Successive State Department International Religious Freedom reports have noted that the U.S. government discusses religious freedom with the [Bahraini] government as part of its overall policy to promote human rights. A U.S. Embassy Manama fact sheet on the Embassy website, accessed in September 2013, notes that the United States funds a judicial reform program to improve the transparency of the judicial system, and that the embassy works with the Ministry of Justice's Judicial and Legal Studies Institute (JLSI) to conduct specialized training for judges, lawyers, law schools, and the bar association.

---

[24] Department of State. "Remarks With Foreign Minister Al Khalifa After Their Meeting." December 3, 2010.

Other Human Rights Issues[25]

Many of the human rights issues in Bahrain are directly tied to the schism between the Sunni-led regime and the Shiite majority, as noted in reports on human rights and religious freedom in Bahrain, such as the State Department report and reports by Human Rights Watch and other groups. The reports also note problems for non-Muslims and for non-Shiite opponents of the government, as well as limitations in the rights of laborers and labor unions.

There are several Bahraini human rights groups, mainly advocates for Shiite rights and causes. The most prominent are the Bahrain Human Rights Society (the primary licensed human rights organization), the Bahrain Transparency Society, and the Bahrain Center for Human Rights (BCHR) and its offshoot, the Bahrain Youth Society for Human Rights (BYSHR). The latter organization was officially dissolved but remain active informally. As noted above, the government has arrested several leaders of these organizations.

U.N. Scrutiny

Bahrain has drawn increasing attention from U.N. human rights bodies and other governments. On June 28, 2012, 28 countries issued a joint declaration, during U.N. Human Rights Council debate, condemning human rights abuses by the Bahrain government. The United States, Britain, and eight other EU countries did not support the initiative. Human rights groups criticized the Administration for refusing to block the September 28, 2012, vote in the U.N. Human Rights Council to fill one of its advisory committee vacancies with a Bahraini representative, Saeed Mohammad al-Faihani. That vote came nine days after the Human Rights Council accepted a Universal Periodic Review of Bahrain's human rights record, in which the government agreed to fully accept 140 out of 176 recommendations of the review. In early December 2012, a team from the United Nations Human Rights Council visited Bahrain to assess the human rights situation; it met with the government as well as the opposition. On September 9, 2013, 47 countries, including the United States, joined the U.N. Office of the High Commissioner for Human Rights in stating that the human rights situation in Bahrain remains an issue of serious concern.[26] Opposition activists reportedly have requested that the U.N. team recommended the appointment of a Special Rapporteur on human rights in Bahrain, and the establishment of a formal U.N. office in Bahrain that would monitor human rights practices there. That step has not been taken, to date.

---

[25] Much of this section is from the State Department's country report on human rights practices for 2012 (released April 19, 2013), http://www.state.gov/j/drl/rls/hrrpt/humanrightsreport/index htm?year=2012&dlid=204370#wrapper; the *International Religious Freedom Report* for 2012 (May 20, 2013), http://www.state.gov/j/drl/rls/irf/religiousfreedom/index.htm?year=2012&dlid=208398#wrapper; and the *Trafficking in Persons Report for 2013* (June 19, 2013), http://www.state.gov/documents/organization/210740.pdf. See also: Human Rights Watch: World Report 2014.

[26] http://pomed.org/wordpress/wp-content/uploads/Joint-Statement-on-the-OHCHR-and-the-human-rights-situation-in-Bahrain-FINAL.pdf?utm_source=Project+on+Middle+East+Democracy+-+All+Contacts&utm_campaign=52543e5858-Bahrain_Weekly_Update_Nov_1_2012&utm_medium=email&utm_term=0_75a06056d7-52543e5858-215946089.

Women's Rights

Bahrain has tended to be relatively progressive as far as law and regulations. However, as is the case with its neighbors, Bahrain's practices and customs tend to limit women's rights. Women can drive, own and inherit property, and initiate divorce cases, although religious courts may refuse a woman's divorce request. Some prominent women are campaigning for a codified family law that would enhance and secure women's rights, running into opposition from Bahraini clerics who are against granting more rights for women. The campaign for the law is backed by King Hamad's wife, Shaykha Sabeeka, and the Supreme Council for Women, which is one association that promotes women's rights in Bahrain. Others include the Bahrain Women's Union, the Bahrain Women's Association, and the Young Ladies Association.

To try to showcase its progressiveness, the government has promoted several women to high positions. The number of women in both chambers of the National Assembly is provided in **Table 1**, above. Since 2005, there have been at least two female ministers—Minister of Human Rights and Social Development Fatima bint Ahmad al-Balushi and Minister of Information and Culture Mai bint Muhammad Al Khalifa. A third female, Samira Rajab, was added to the cabinet in 2012 as minister of state for media affairs. Huda Azar Nonoo, an attorney and formerly the only Jew in the Shura Council, has been ambassador to the United States since 2008, although a male has been named to replace her. As noted above, a female—Dana Zayani—heads the "Follow Up Unit" that is continuing to oversee implementation of the BICI recommendations.

Religious Freedom

The State Department report on international religious freedom for 2012 (released May 20, 2013) says that the "trend in the government's respect for religious freedom did not change significantly during the year." As in past State Department religious freedom reports on Bahrain, the report for 2012 focuses extensively on Sunni-Shiite differences and the unrest. According to past State Department reports on religious freedom in Bahrain, the government allows freedom of worship for Christians, Jews, and Hindus although the constitution declares Islam the official religion. Non-Muslim groups must register with the Ministry of Social Development to operate and 19 non-Muslim religious groups are registered as of the end of 2012, including Christian churches and a Hindu temple. During 2012, the government donated land for the Roman Catholic Vicariate of Northern Arabia to relocate from Kuwait to Bahrain.

The Baha'i faith, declared blasphemous in Iran and Afghanistan, has been discriminated against in Bahrain, although recent State Department human rights reports say that the Baha'i community can gather and operates openly. According to the State Department human rights report for 2011, there are about 40 Jews in Bahrain, and no recent reports of anti-Semitic acts.

Aside from sectarian differences, religious conservatives, both Sunni and Shiite, are active in Bahrain. On September 14, 2012, about 2,000 Bahrainis demonstrated in the mostly Shiite district of Diraz against the U.S.-produced video "The Innocence of Muslims." Similar demonstrations took place throughout the Middle East and South Asia.

Media Freedoms

Media freedoms have been curbed since the uprising began. The State Department human rights report for 2012 states that, during 2012, the government suppressed critical speech. In April 2013, the government increased the recommended jail sentence for "insulting the King" to five years, from two years.

Labor Rights

On labor issues, Bahrain has been credited with significant labor reforms, including a 2002 law granting workers, including noncitizens, the right to form and join unions. The law holds that the right to strike is a legitimate means for workers to defend their rights and interests, but their right is restricted in practice, including a prohibition on strikes in the oil and gas, education, and health sectors. There are about 50 trade unions in Bahrain, but all unions must join the General Federation of Bahrain Trade Unions (GFBTU). As a sign of the degree to which the GFBTU is dominated by oppositionists, during the height of unrest in 2011, the GFBTU called at least two general strikes to protest excessive force by security forces. In apparent retaliation by the government and employers, during March-May 2011, employers dismissed almost 2,500 workers from the private sector, and almost 2,000 from the public sector, including 25% of the country's union leadership.

Human Trafficking

On human trafficking, the State Department "Trafficking in Persons Report" for 2013, released June 19, 2013, again places Bahrain in "Tier 2: Watch List." This is the second year in a row that Bahrain is rated at that level—a downgrade from the Tier 2 placement of the 2011 report. The Tier 2 Watch List ranking is based on the government's failure to demonstrate increasing effort to address the human trafficking issue. The report for 2013 asserts that Bahrain is a destination country for migrant workers from India, Pakistan, Nepal, Sri Lanka, Bangladesh, Indonesia, Thailand, the Phillipines, Ethiopia, Ghana, and Eritrea to be subjected to forced labor and sex trafficking.

Executions and Torture

Another issue that has been widely discussed in the context of the uprising, but which predated it, is that of executions and torture. Human Rights Watch and other groups long asserted that Bahrain had been going against the international trend of ending executions. In November 2009, Bahrain's Court of Cassation upheld the sentencing to death by firing squad of a citizen of Bangladesh. That sentenced was imposed for a 2005 murder. From 1977 until 2006, there were no executions in Bahrain.

Allegations of torture against Shiite opposition figures have been widespread. In February 2010, more than one year before the uprising began, Human Rights Watch issued a study alleging systematic use by Bahraini security forces of torture.[27] Witnesses at the May 13, 2011, hearing of the Tom Lantos Human Rights Commission asserted that torture was being used regularly on those (mostly Shiites) arrested in the unrest. The State Department human rights report for 2011 said there were numerous reports of torture and other cruel punishments during the state of emergency (March-June 2011). The government cancelled the planned late May 2013 visit of the U.N. Special Rapporteur on Torture and Other Cruel, Inhuman or Degrading Treatment or Punishment, Juan Mendez—the second cancellation of his visit since the unrest began. Mendez

---

[27] Human Rights Watch. "Bahrain: Torture Redux." February 2010.

said he was "deeply disappointed" in the postponement. On June 7, 2013, 20 Senators and Representatives signed a letter to the King urging him to allow a visit by Mendez in order to demonstrate Bahrain's "commitment to help put an end to such abuses."[28]

U.S.-Bahrain Security and Foreign Policy Relations[29]

The U.S.-Bahrain security relationship dates to the end of World War II and, since the late 1970s, defense and security issues have been central to U.S.-Bahrain relations. In large part to keep powerful neighbors in check, Bahrain has linked its security to the United States, and has placed its facilities at U.S. disposal to address threats from Iraq, Iran, Afghanistan, international terrorism, and piracy in the Gulf and Arabia Sea. Bahrain, as much as any GCC state, considers Iran's nuclear program a major potential threat. Since the U.S.-led ousting of Saddam Hussein in Iraq, the perceived threat from Iraq has receded because Iraq's military is far smaller and less well-armed than it was during the rule of Saddam Hussein.

In addition to the long-standing U.S. naval headquarters presence in Bahrain, the two countries signed a formal Defense Cooperation Agreement (DCA) in 1991. In March 2002, President Bush (Presidential Determination 2002-10) designated Bahrain a "major non-NATO ally (MNNA)," a designation that qualifies Bahrain to purchase the same U.S. arms that NATO allies can purchase.

However, since the Bahrain uprising began in 2011, Bahrain-U.S. political relations have been somewhat strained. U.S. officials say that U.S.- Bahrain defense cooperation has not suffered significantly, although the Bahrain government has become slightly less forthcoming with in-kind support to the U.S. military presence in Bahrain than it was before the unrest began. U.S. officials add that there are few, if any, security cooperation initiatives that the United States can use as leverage to obtain Bahrain government flexibility on the unrest issue.

The opposition says that U.S.-Bahrain defense relations are not at risk should the Shiite opposition achieve greater influence in Bahrain; *Wifaq* leader Salman has said in interviews that he supports continuing the security relationship with the United States. Some observers assert that the opposition sees the continued U.S. presence in Bahrain as leverage the United States can use to persuade the Bahraini government to offer concessions to the opposition. Others observers say that opposition figures privately maintain that, were the opposition to come to power, the U.S. military would be expelled from Bahrain.

U.S. Naval Headquarters in Bahrain

The cornerstone of U.S.-Bahrain defense relations is U.S. access to Bahrain's naval facilities. February 2008 marked the 60th anniversary of a U.S. naval command presence in Bahrain; MIDEASTFOR (U.S. Middle East Force), its successor, NAVCENT (naval component of U.S. Central Command), as well as the Fifth Fleet (reconstituted in June 1995) are headquartered there, at a sprawling facility called "Naval Support Activity-Bahrain." The facility, along with

---

[28] http://www.humanrightsfirst.org/wp-content/uploads/HRF-King-Al-Khalifa-Letter.pdf.

[29] Information in this section obtained from a variety of press reports, and the Defense Security Cooperation Agency (DSCA).

others, accommodates 7,000 U.S. personnel, mostly Navy, deployed in Bahrain.[30] It is also home to U.S. Marine Forces Central Command, Destroyer Squadron Fifty, and three Combined Maritime Forces.[31] The "on-shore" U.S. command presence in Bahrain was established after the 1991 Gulf war against Iraq; prior to that, the U.S. naval headquarters in Bahrain was on a command ship mostly docked in Bahrain and technically "off shore."

Some smaller U.S. ships (e.g., minesweepers) are home-ported there, but the Fifth Fleet consists mostly of U.S.-homeported ships that are sent to the region on six- to seven-month deployments. Ships operating in the Fifth Fleet at any given time typically include a carrier strike group, an amphibious ready group, and some additional surface combatants, and operate in both the Persian Gulf and Indian Ocean/Northern Arabian Sea. In mid-March 2012, the U.S. Navy announced it was doubling its minesweepers in the Gulf to eight, and sending additional mine-hunting helicopters, as tensions escalated over Iran's nuclear program and its threatened reaction to new sanctions. In May 2013, the U.S. Navy announced it is moving an additional five coastal patrol ships to Bahrain, to join five already there. The naval headquarters serves as the command headquarters for periodic exercises intended to signal resolve to Iran; a mine-sweeping exercise involving 41 countries was held in the Gulf during May 5-30, 2013.

The naval headquarters also coordinates the operations of over 20 U.S. and allied warships in Combined Task Force (CTF) 151 and 152 that seek to interdict the movement of terrorists, pirates, arms, or weapons of mass destruction (WMD)-related technology and narcotics across the Arabian Sea. In March 2008, Bahrain took a turn in a rotation to command CTF-152, and it commanded again in December 2010. Bahrain commanded an anti-piracy task force in Gulf/Arabian Sea waters in October 2010. These operations are offshoots of Operation Enduring Freedom (OEF) in Afghanistan, which ousted the Taliban after the September 11 attacks.

To further develop the naval facility (sometimes referred to as "Bahrain Island"), and other military facilities, the U.S. military is implementing a planned $580 million military construction program in Bahrain.[32] That construction, which began in May 2010, will add 77 acres (the decommissioned Mina (port) Al Salman Pier, leased by the Navy under a January 2008 lease agreement) to the existing 80 acre facility. When completed in 2017, the expansion will provide a new administration building and additional space for maintenance, barracks, warehousing, and dining facilities. The expansion will support the deployment of additional U.S. coastal patrol ships and the Navy's new littoral combat ship, and permit larger U.S. ships to dock at the naval facility.[33] A separate deep water port in Bahrain, Khalifa bin Salman, is one of the few facilities in the Gulf that can accommodate U.S. aircraft carriers and amphibious ships.[34]

Of the military construction program under way in Bahrain, $45 million is being used to expand an apron at Shaykh Isa Air Base, where a variety of U.S. aircraft are stationed, including F-16s, F-

---

[30] Hendrick Simoes. "Bahrain Expansion Latest Sign of Continued Presence." Stars and Stripes, December 16, 2013.

[31] For an extended discussion of the U.S. military presence in Bahrain, see Brookings Institution, Center for 21st Century Security and Intelligence, Policy Paper "No 'Plan B': U.S. Strategic Access in the Middle East and the Question of Bahrain. June 2013, by Commander Richard McDaniel, U.S.N.

[32] Among the recent appropriations to fund the expansion are: $54 million for FY2008 (Division 1 of P.L. 110-161); $41.5 million for FY2010 (P.L. 111-117); $258 million for FY2011 (P.L. 112-10). $100 million was requested for FY2012 for two projects, but was not funded in the FY2012 Consolidated Appropriation (P.L. 112-74).

[33] Hendrick Simoes. "Bahrain Expansion Latest Sign of Continued Presence." Stars and Stripes, December 16, 2013.

[34] Ibid.

18s, and P-3 surveillance aircraft. About $19 million is to be used for a Special Operations Forces facility.

Some say that the United States should begin examining alternate facilities in the Gulf region in the expectation that continued Bahraini hosting of the U.S. naval headquarters has become unstable. On July 22, 2011, the U.S. Navy in Bahrain issued a statement refuting a British press report that the Navy is planning to relocate the facility. Should there be a decision to take that step, likely alternatives in the Gulf would include Qatar's New Doha Port (to open in 2016), Kuwait's Shuaiba port, and the UAE's Jebel Ali.[35] None of these countries has publicly expressed a position on whether it would be willing to host such an expanded facility, but they have been highly cooperative with U.S. defense efforts in the Gulf and presumably would be willing to host the naval headquarters. U.S. officials say other Gulf state facilities, such as Jebel Ali in UAE, do not currently provide large U.S. ships with the ease of docking access that Bahrain does, and that many of the alternative possibilities inconveniently share docking and other facilities with large commercial operations. Such facilities could be improved, if necessary, by further construction.

Defense Cooperation Agreement (DCA)

Bahrain was part of the U.S.-led allied coalition that ousted Iraq from Kuwait in 1991, beyond the hosting of the U.S. naval headquarters. Bahrain allowed the stationing of 17,500 U.S. troops and 250 U.S. combat aircraft at Shaykh Isa Air Base that participated in the Desert Storm offensive against Iraqi forces. Bahrain and the United States subsequently decided to institutionalize that expanded cooperation by signing a Defense Cooperation Agreement (DCA) on October 28, 1991, for an initial period of ten years. The DCA remains in effect.[36] The pact reportedly not only provides the United States access to Bahrain's air bases and to pre-position strategic materiel (mostly U.S. Air Force munitions), but also requires consultations with Bahrain if its security is threatened, and it expanded exercises and U.S. training of Bahraini forces.[37] The pact encompasses a "Status of Forces Agreement" (SOFA) under which U.S. military personnel serving in Bahrain operate under U.S., and not Bahraini, law.

Under the DCA, there were about 1,300 U.S. military personnel in Bahrain during the 1990s to contain Saddam Hussein's Iraq, and Bahraini pilots flew strikes over Iraq during the war; Iraq fired nine Scud missiles at Bahrain during the war, of which three hit facilities there. Bahrain hosted the regional headquarters for U.N. weapons inspections in Iraq during 1991-1998, and the U.S.-led Multinational Interdiction Force (MIF) that enforced a U.N. embargo on Iraq during 1991-2003. Since the early 1990s, the United States has reportedly stationed two Patriot anti-missile batteries there.[38]

Bahrain allowed the United States to fly combat missions from its bases (Shaykh Isa Air Base) in both Operation Enduring Freedom (OEF) in Afghanistan and the war to oust Saddam Hussein in

---

[35] Ibid.

[36] "U.S.-Bahrain Defense Pact Renewed." *Agence France Presse*, August 5, 2011.

[37] Details of the U.S.-Bahrain defense agreement are classified. Some provisions are discussed in Sami Hajjar, *U.S. Military Presence in the Gulf: Challenges and Prospects* (U.S. Army War College: Strategic Studies Institute), March 2002, p. 27. The State and Defense Departments have not provided CRS with requested information on the duration of the pact, or whether its terms had been modified in recent years.

[38] Walter Pincus. "Bahrain Government's Ties With the United States Run Deep." *Washington Post*, February 22, 2011.

March-April 2003 (Operation Iraqi Freedom, OIF). During both OEF and OIF, Bahrain publicly deployed its U.S.-supplied frigate warship (the *Subha*) to help protect U.S. ships, and it sent ground and air assets to Kuwait in support of OIF. Bahrain hosted about 4,000 U.S. military personnel during major combat of OEF (October 2001-May 2003).

Bahrain and UAE have been the only Gulf states to deploy their own forces to provide aid to Afghanistan. In January 2009, Bahrain sent 100 police officers to Afghanistan on a two-year tour to help U.S./NATO-led stabilization operations there. Their tour was extended until the end of the NATO mission at the end of 2014.

U.S. Arms Transfers and Military Aid

To assist Bahrain's ability to cooperate with the United States on regional security issues, the United States has taken into consideration Bahrain's limited financial resources and provided small amounts of military assistance. Because U.S. military aid has been relatively small, Bahrain has mostly used national funds to buy the $1.4 billion worth of U.S. weaponry it bought from 2000-2013.[39] The unrest has caused the Administration to put on hold sales to Bahrain equipment that could easily be used against protesters, while continuing to provide equipment that is suited to Bahrain's external defense capabilities and its support for U.S. operations in the region. Sales of small arms are generally commercial sales, licensed by State Department with Defense Department concurrence. On September 10, 2011, the State Department licensed a sale of 250 pistols to the Bahrain Defense Force (BDF) and other firearms for the protection of a high ranking Bahraini official. Since 2012, the department has put "on hold" license requests for sales to Bahrain of small arms, light weapons, and ammunition.[40]

The main recipient of U.S. military assistance has been the relatively small BDF—Bahrain's military force—which has less than 10,000 active duty personnel, including 1,200 National Guard. The BDF, as well as Bahrain's police forces, are run by Sunni Bahrainis, but supplement their ranks with unknown percentages of paid recruits from Sunni Muslim neighboring countries, including Pakistan, Yemen, Jordan, Iraq, and elsewhere. Some human rights groups say that BDF equipment, such as Cobra helicopters, have been used against protesters and that the United States cannot be sure that sales to and training of the BDF is not being used to crush unrest.

Foreign Military Financing (FMF)

Foreign Military Financing (FMF) was suspended for Bahrain in FY1994 but restarted in appreciation of Bahrain's support in OEF and OIF. According to the Administration, FMF (and funds provided under "Section 1206" of the National Defense Authorization Act of 2006, P.L. 109-163) is provided to Bahrain to help it maintain U.S.-origin weapons, to enhance inter-operability with U.S. forces, to augment Bahrain's air defenses, to support and upgrade the avionics of its F-16 combat aircraft (see below), and to improve counterterrorism capabilities. As an example, the United States has supplied Bahrain with a coastal radar system that reportedly provides Bahrain and the U.S. Navy a 360-degree field of vision around Bahrain.[41] Some FMF

---

[39] Justin Elliott. "Revealed: America's Arms Sales to Bahrain Amid Bloody Crackdown." Propublica, January 15, 2013.

[40] Email from the Office of the Assistant Secretary of Defense for Legislative Affairs, May 20, 2013.

[41] "Bahrain Government's Ties With the United States Run Deep," op. cit.

funds have been used to build up Bahrain's Special Operations forces and, in April 2012, U.S. military teams reportedly provided additional training to the BDF on the use of its Blackhawk helicopters.[42] The Defense Department estimates that, in part due to U.S. assistance, about 50% of Bahrain's forces are fully capable of integrating into a U.S.-led coalition.

The Administration's FY2012 aid request, made at the start of the unrest, asked for $25 million in FMF for Bahrain. As shown in **Table 4** below, only $10 million was provided for FY2012, due in large part to the Administration's intent to retain leverage against Bahrain to compel it to make reforms. The same lower amount, $10 million, was provided for FY2013 and is expected to be provided in FY2014.

Excess Defense Articles (EDA)

Bahrain is eligible to receive grant "excess defense articles" (EDA), and it has received over $400 million worth of EDA since the program began for Bahrain in 1993. In June 1995, the United States provided 50 M-60A3 tanks to Bahrain as a "no cost" five-year lease. Bahrain later received title to the equipment. In July 1997, the United States transferred the FFG-7 "Perry class" frigate *Subha* (see above) as EDA. In the State Department's FY2012 budget request, the Administration supported providing another frigate (an "extended deck frigate") to Bahrain as EDA because the *Subha* is approaching the end of its service life. The Administration said on May 11, 2012, that it continued to support that transfer, which is planned for 2014, subject to passage of authorizing legislation.[43] However, the FY2014 foreign aid budget justification says that the BDF has put acquisition of a new frigate on hold, and would put U.S. military aid toward maintaining the *Subha* instead.

International Military Education and Training Funds (IMET)

As noted in **Table 4**, small amounts of International Military Education and Training funds (IMET) are provided to Bahrain to inculcate principles of civilian control of the military, democracy, and interoperability with U.S. forces. Approximately 250 Bahraini military students attend U.S. military schools each year, either through the IMET program (57% of them), or using FMF funds, in connection with the U.S. Foreign Military Sales program.

Major Foreign Military Sales (FMS) From Bahrain National Funds

Bahrain's total government budget is about $6 billion per year, allowing modest amounts of national funds to be used for purchases of major combat systems. In 1998, Bahrain purchased 10 U.S.-made F-16Cs from new production, worth about $390 million. It later purchased 12 more of the system, bringing its F-16 fleet to 22. In 1999, the United States sold Bahrain 26 Advanced Medium-Range Air-to-Air Missiles (AMRAAM) to arm the F-16s.

An August 2000 sale of 30 Army Tactical Missile Systems (ATACMs, a system of short-range ballistic missiles fired from a multiple rocket launcher), valued at about $70 million, included an agreement for joint U.S.-Bahraini control of the weapon. That arrangement was reached in part to allay U.S. congressional concerns about possible U.S. promotion of missile proliferation in the

---

[42] "Revealed: America's Arms Sales to Bahrain Amid Bloody Crackdown," op.cit.

[43] http://www.state.gov/r/pa/prs/ps/2012/05/189810 htm.

region. Sales of up to 180 "Javelin" anti-armor missiles and 60 launch units, worth up to $42 million; 9 UH-60M Blackhawk helicopters worth up to $252 million; and 6 Bell search and recovery helicopters, valued at about $160 million, were notified August 3, 2007. An additional 25 AMRAAMs (Raytheon Missile Systems Corp.) and associated equipment, valued at about $74 million, was notified for sale to Bahrain on July 28, 2009. Section 581 of the FY1990 foreign operations appropriation act (P.L. 101-167) made Bahrain the only Gulf state eligible to receive the Stinger shoulder-fired anti-aircraft missile, and the United States has sold Bahrain about 70 Stingers since 1990. (This authorization has been repeated in subsequent legislation.)

Some of the recent sales to Bahrain are in accordance with the State Department's "Gulf Security Dialogue," begun in 2006 to counter Iran. Much of the initiative involves missile defense integration, and it is primarily Bahrain's wealthier neighbors, such as UAE, that are buying advanced U.S. missile defense equipment. That prevents Bahrain from becoming a major factor in the U.S. effort to assemble a Gulf-wide, integrated missile defense network. That effort has been discussed extensively with the Gulf states; on March 31, 2012, then Secretary of State Clinton attended the first ministerial meeting of the U.S.-GCC Strategic Cooperation Forum in Riyadh, Saudi Arabia, which focused on the integrated Gulf missile defense plan. Subsequently, Deputy Assistant Secretary of State Frank Rose spoke in Abu Dhabi on April 12, 2012,[44] on that issue. The concept was also discussed between the United States and the GCC countries at a meeting on the sidelines of the U.N. General Assembly meetings in September 2012.

September 2011 Humvee and TOW Sale

One sale, notified on September 14, 2011, was announced seven months after the unrest began, and has been agreed to despite U.S. criticism of Bahrain's crackdown. It is for a proposed sale of 44 "Humvee" (M115A1B2) armored vehicles and several hundred TOW missiles of various models, of which 50 are to be "bunker busters." Along with associated equipment and support, the proposed sale is worth an estimated $53 million. Although not considered large in dollar terms, or of particularly sophisticated equipment, the sale incurred opposition from several human rights groups and from the Bahraini opposition who assert that the sale represents U.S. downplaying of the abuses committed by the Bahraini government in the course of the unrest. Human rights groups and Bahraini opposition figures say the regime could use the Humvees, in particular, in their efforts to crack down on protests. When the sale was announced, State Department officials said the sale would not violate the intent of the "Leahy amendment"—a provision of foreign aid and defense appropriations laws that forbids U.S. sales of equipment to security units that have committed human rights abuses.[45]

Two joint resolutions were introduced in the 112th Congress to block the sale: S.J.Res. 28, introduced by Senator Ron Wyden, and H.J.Res. 80, introduced by Representative James McGovern. Both joint resolutions would have prohibited the sale unless the Administration certifies that Bahrain is rectifying the alleged abuses connected to its suppression of the uprising in 2011. To block a proposed arms sale would require passage of a joint resolution to do so, and with a veto-proof majority, because President Obama could veto a joint resolution of disapproval in order to complete the sale. The House bill attracted 14 co-sponsors, the Senate bill 2 co-sponsors. On October 19, 2011, even though the sale had passed the period of congressional

---

[44] U.S. Department of State Daily Digest Bulletin, April 12, 2012.

[45] James Lobe. "Bahrain: U.S. Congress Urged to Reject Arms Sales." IPS News Service, September 29, 2011.

review, and apparently addressing the criticism and legislative initiatives, the Administration told Congress it would delay the sale until it could review the BICI report that was released November 23, 2011. Still, the State Department spokesperson stated on January 27, 2012, that "we are maintaining a pause on most security assistance to Bahrain pending further progress on reform." At the same briefing, the department said it was releasing to Bahrain previously notified and cleared spare parts and maintenance—worth a reported $1 million—needed for Bahrain's external defense and support of Fifth Fleet operations. None of the items can be used against protesters, according to the State Department statement.[46]

May 11, 2012 Resumption of Some Arms Sales[47]

As discussed above, on May 11, 2012, in conjunction with a visit to Washington, DC, by Bahrain's Crown Prince Salman, the Administration announced that, despite continuing concerns about Bahrain's handling of the unrest, it would open up Bahrain to the purchase of additional U.S. arms for the BDF, Bahrain's Coast Guard, and Bahrain's National Guard. The Administration stated that the weaponry that would be sold is not typically used in crowd control or riot control, and that the TOW and Humvee sale discussed, as well as any sales of equipment that could be used against protesters (tear gas and rifles, for example), would remain on hold. The Administration did not release a complete list of weapons to be sold, but it gave a few examples as follows:

- The Perry-class frigate, as EDA, discussed above; but later mooted;
- Harbor security boats for the Bahrain Coast Guard, as EDA;
- An upgrade to the engines on Bahrain's U.S.-made F-16s; and
- Additional AMRAAMs (see above), according to press reports quoting U.S. officials knowledgeable about the decision.[48]

Some Members of Congress publicly criticized the May 11, 2012, decision as yielding U.S. leverage on the government to enact more substantial reforms. Some said they might seek legislation to block the proposed sales,[49] but no such legislation was enacted. However, subsequently, in a provision that appears in large part directed at U.S. arms sales policy toward Bahrain, a provision of the FY2014 Consolidated Appropriation (P.L. 113-76) prohibits use of U.S. funds for "tear gas, small arms, light weapons, ammunition, or other items for crowd control purposes for foreign security forces that use excessive force to repress peaceful expression, association, or assembly in countries undergoing democratic transition."

Anti-Terrorism Cooperation

Mostly prior to the 2011 uprising, the United States provided some assistance to Ministry of Interior-supervised internal security forces to facilitate their cooperation with regional U.S. counterterrorism operations. Since the uprising began, U.S. aid to the Interior Ministry-controlled forces has become controversial because of the role of these forces in suppressing the unrest.

---

[46] Department of State. Taken Question: Bahrain's Security Assistance. January 27, 2012.

[47] http://www.state.gov/r/pa/prs/ps/2012/05/189810 htm.

[48] Nicole Gaouette. "U.S. Resumes Bahrain Arms Sales Citing Security Interests." Bloomberg News, May 11, 2012.

[49] Sara Sorcher. "Arms Sales to Bahrain Anger Senators." National Journal Daily, May 14, 2012.

Until 1998, Bahrain's internal security services were run by a former British colonial police officer, Ian Henderson, who had a reputation among Shiites for using repressive measures. And, the current director of the internal security service is Shaykh Khalifa bin Abdullah Al Khalifa, considered a hardliner in the royal family.

The United States has worked with Bahrain's Interior Ministry on counter-terrorism issues, but cooperation has been affected somewhat by the uprising. According to the FY2012 budget justification, the Administration was "reviewing" the use of NADR-ATA support to Bahrain to ensure that none was used "against protestors" in the 2011 unrest. The FY2013 budget justification said that NADR-ATA support would continue to go to the Ministry of Interior "on a limited basis," and in part to prod the ministry on security sector reform and implementation of the BICI recommendations. The State Department, as noted above, has placed on hold license requests for small arms and related equipment to the Bahraini government in general. The FY2014 budget justification stressed that NADR-ATA will focus on helping security forces counter the explosive devices used by extremist elements within the opposition—suggesting that the Administration shares the Bahrain government's view that the opposition is increasingly developing a violent component. As noted by the State Department, some of the NADR-ATA funds have previously been used to provide training to its counterterrorism institutions, to augment the ability of Bahraini forces to protect U.S. diplomatic and military facilities in Bahrain, and to help train Bahrain's police contingent in Afghanistan guard Camp Leatherneck in Helmand Province.

The State Department's report on international terrorism for 2011 (released July 31, 2012) noted some of the government responses to the BICI report, particularly ending the National Security Agency's arrest and detention authorities. The State Department report on terrorism for 2012 (released May 30, 2013), said the agency had transferred those authorities to the Ministry of Interior in 2012.[50]

Regarding regional anti-terrorism cooperation, the State Department terrorism report for 2012 continues to credit Bahrain with strongly cooperating with U.S. and international counterterrorism efforts. Bahrain has hosted the Middle East and North Africa Financial Action Task Force (MENA/FATF) secretariat, and its Central Bank, Financial Information Unit (within the Central Bank), and local banks have cooperated with U.S. efforts against terrorism financing and money laundering.

Foreign Policy Issues

Bahrain relies on its relations with the Gulf Cooperation Council (GCC) states to protect it from the internal threat to the ruling family. It relies on the United States, primarily, to protect it from the external threat from Iran.

GCC/Saudi Arabia

Bahrain has close relations with the other GCC states, and in particular Saudi Arabia, as evidenced by the Saudi intervention in Bahrain in 2011. Virtually all the GCC states have political structures similar to that of Bahrain, and several have substantial Shiite minorities, although none

---

[50] http://www.state.gov/j/ct/rls/crt/2012/209982 htm.

of the others has a Shiite majority. Many Saudis visit Bahrain on weekends to enjoy the relatively more liberal social atmosphere there and escape the restrictions of their own country; to do so, Saudis cross a causeway constructed in 1986 that connects it to Bahrain. That highway links to the eastern provinces of Saudi Arabia, where most of the Kingdom's Shiites (about 10% of the population) live. Among all the other linkages, King Hamad's fifth son, Khalid bin Hamad, married a daughter of Saudi King Abdullah in 2011. Since the beginning of the Bahrain unrest, Saudi Arabia reportedly has donated at least $500 million to help Bahrain's economy.

Well before intervening in Bahrain, the GCC states, particularly Saudi Arabia, had begun to fear that the Bahrain unrest could spread to other GCC states and that Iran could exploit the situation in Bahrain. ing Saudi Arabia, have substantial Shiite minorities. The Saudi position is that it will not, under any circumstances, permit a Shiite takeover in Bahrain, and the Saudi government is seen as backing hardline, anti-compromise officials in the Bahrain ruling family.

To reinforce its stance on Bahrain, on May 14, 2012, Saudi Arabia and Bahrain announced they supported a plan to form a close political and military union among the GCC states ("Riyadh Declaration")—a signal to Bahrain's Shiite opposition that the Bahrain government has unconditional Saudi backing. At a GCC leadership meeting in Riyadh that day, the other four GCC states opposed such a union and the GCC as a whole formally deferred a decision on the Saudi-Bahraini plan. Still, the GCC states agreed in December 2012 to a collective security agreement that combats crime and terrorism through information exchanges. Bahrain's cabinet endorsed the agreement on December 30, 2012. Opposition from some GCC states, particularly Oman, blocked agreement on the political unification plan again at the GCC summit in Kuwait during December 10-11, 2013.

Because of historic ties between their two royal families, Kuwait has sometimes been touted as a potential mediator in the Bahraini political crisis. Both royal families hail from the Anizah tribe that settled in Bahrain and some of whom went on to what is now Kuwait. Kuwaiti Shiites in Kuwait's parliament have argued against Kuwait's siding firmly with the Al Khalifa regime. However, the Kuwaiti government did, as noted with its naval deployments, join the GCC position on the side of the government and it is giving financial aid to Bahrain.

Bahrain has stayed within a GCC consensus on regional issues, although Bahrain's resource constraints—and focus on the internal situation—prevent it from taking as active a role as Saudi Arabia, UAE, or Qatar. Bahrain did not play a significant role in assisting the Libyan opposition to the rule of Muammar Al Qadhafi. Had Bahrain intervened in Libya, doing so could have been viewed as a contradiction—supporting a revolutionary movement in another Arab state while arguing that its domestic opposition's grievances lacked legitimacy. As part of the GCC, Bahrain also joined the GCC efforts, which yielded success in November 2011, to persuade Yemen's President Ali Abdullah Saleh to cede power to a transition process. He left Yemen in January 2012.

The GCC as a whole, and perhaps Bahrain most acutely, sees Syria as Iran's main Middle Eastern ally and seeks the ouster of President Bashar Al Assad. In August 2011, Bahrain joined the other GCC countries in withdrawing their ambassadors to Syria. In November 2011, the GCC voted with other Arab League states to suspend Syria's membership in the body. In April 2012, the GCC states also proposed giving the Syrian opposition $100 million in funding that it can use to buy weaponry, although most of that funding reportedly is being provided by the UAE, Qatar, Kuwait, and Saudi Arabia. Some of the GCC states, but not Bahrain, are said to be providing weapons as well. Since June 2013, Bahrain has joined its GCC partners in threatening to expel sympathizers of Lebanese Hezbollah following Hezbollah's confirmation of its entry into the Syria conflict on Assad's side.

Relations with and Cooperation Against Iran

Bahrain focuses its foreign policy intently on Iran, which the government asserts is supporting Shiite opposition groups. Bahrain has supported U.S. and international efforts to increase economic pressure on Iran to compel it to limit its nuclear program. In a joint news conference with then Secretary Clinton on December 3, 2010, referenced earlier, Bahrain's foreign minister restated Bahrain's support for Iran's right to nuclear power for peaceful uses, but that "when it comes to taking that [nuclear] power, to developing it into a cycle for weapon grade, that is something that we can never accept, and we can never live with in this region."[51] Bahrain tepidly supported publicly the November 24, 2013, interim nuclear agreement between Iran and the international community, calling it "consistent with [Bahrain's] stances and policies which advocate diplomatic solutions to maintain stability." However, some reports say the deal has caused U.S.-Bahrain government friction in that Bahrain's leaders are apparently concerned the deal will cause the United States to ease economic pressure on Iran and potentially reduce its commitment to the security of the Gulf. This might explain Secretary of Defense Hagel's December 7, 2013, speech at the Manama Dialogue in which he attempted to reassure Bahrain and all the GCC states of U.S. resolve to maintain the security of the region. Bahrain and Saudi Arabia were the only two GCC states that did not host a visit by Iranian Foreign Minister Mohammad Javad Zarif or his associates after the interim nuclear agreement was signed.

As noted, Bahraini leaders have consistently asserted that Iran is actively stoking the Bahrain unrest. On March 21, 2011, King Hamad indirectly accused Iran of involvement in the unrest by saying a "foreign plot" had been foiled by the GCC intervention. Iran and Bahrain withdrew their ambassadors in mid-March 2011, but returned them in August 2012. On February 21, 2013, the government said that Iran's Revolutionary guard had helped form a Bahraini cell—part of a group called the "Imam Army"—to recruit other agents and store weapons in Bahrain for possible attacks on officials and key locations.[52] In May 2013, the government declared Lebanese Hezbollah a terrorist organization, accusing that organization of helping orchestrate a Shiite-led insurgency in Bahrain.[53] Bahrain's accusations against Iran and Hezbollah, have not changed since the August 4, 2013, inauguration of Iran's relatively moderate President Hassan Rouhani. Bahraini authorities used the ship interception of December 2013, discussed above, to underscore their point about Iranian support for radical Bahrain oppositionists.

U.S. officials publicly differ, although not dramatically, with the Bahraini assertions. Ambassador Krajeski testified on September 21, 2011, that the United States "saw no evidence of Iranian instigation" of the unrest, but that the United States is concerned "about Iranian exploitation" of it. U.S. officials reportedly believe that Iran has urged hardline Bahraini Shiite factions not to compromise.[54] On April 14, 2011, U.S. officials, speaking on background, told journalists that there was some information to indicate that Iran might have transferred small amounts of

---

[51] Department of State. Transcript of Remarks by Secretary Clinton and Foreign Minister Al Khalifa. December 3, 2010.

[52] "Iran's Revolutionary guard Behind Terror Cell, Says Bahrain." Saudi Gazette, February 22, 2013.

[53] The United States designated Hezbollah as a Foreign Terrorist Organization, FTO, in 1997 when that list was established by the Immigration and Nationality Act, 8 U.S.C. 1189.

[54] http://www.stripes.com/gates-protracted-bahrain-negotiations-allowing-greater-iran-influence-1.137532.

weapons to Bahraini oppositionists.[55] The BICI report largely absolved Iran of direct involvement in the unrest, although the report blamed Iran's media for incitement of the situation in Bahrain. Since that report, U.S. officials have not directly accused Iran of backing Bahrain's opposition.

Well before the 2011 unrest, Bahrain's fears about Iran had been infused by lingering suspicions, sometimes fed by Iranian actions, that Iran never accepted the results of the 1970 U.N. survey giving Bahrain independence rather than integration with Iran. Those findings were endorsed by U.N. Security Council Resolution 278, which was ratified by Iran's parliament. After these official determinations, Bahrain had considered the issue closed, after over a century of Persian contestation of Bahraini sovereignty. Those contests included an effort by Reza Shah Pahlavi of Iran in the 1930s to deny Bahrain the right to grant oil concessions to the United States and Britain. In December 1981, and then again in June 1996—a time when Iran was actively seeking to export its Islamic revolution—Bahrain publicly accused Iran of trying to organize a coup by pro-Iranian Bahraini Shiites (the Islamic Front for the Liberation of Bahrain, IFLB). The group's successor is the Bahrain Islamic Action Society, which is outlawed. A July 2007 Iranian newspaper article reasserting the Iranian claim to Bahrain. In March 2009, Ali Akbar Nateq Nuri, an advisor to Iran's Supreme Leader, again referred to Bahrain as Iran's 14th province. Iran's Foreign Ministry immediately tried to limit any diplomatic damage by asserting respect for Bahrain's sovereignty and independence, but some Arab governments sharply criticized the comments; Morocco broke relations with Iran.

At the same time, Bahrain, like the other GCC states, tries not to openly or directly antagonize Iran. Bahrain permitted then Iranian President Ahmadinejad to visit Bahrain on November 17, 2007. Despite its political difficulties with Iran, Bahrain maintains normal trade with Iran, probably to avoid antagonizing Iran into undertaking more assertive action on behalf of Bahrain's opposition. There are no indications that Iran-Bahrain general commerce has been affected by the unrest in Bahrain. On the other hand, in mid-September 2012, Bahrain confiscated carbon fiber bound for Iran, an item that could contribute to Iran's nuclear program.

Bahrain generally enforces U.S. sanctions against Iran, largely because the leadership agrees with the strategy underpinning the sanctions. However, some Bahraini firms and traders maintain relations with Iran in order not to harm longstanding trade relationships. Energy market observers say that some Bahrain energy firms may still be supplying gasoline to Iran. No U.N. Security Council Resolution bars such sales, but a U.S. law signed on July 1, 2010—the Comprehensive Iran Sanctions, Accountability, and Divestment Act of 2010 (CISADA, P.L. 111-195)—provides for sanctions against foreign firms that sell more than $1 million worth of gasoline to Iran.[56] No Bahraini gasoline traders have been sanctioned.

Foreign banks that deal with sanctioned Iranian banks or Iran's Central Bank are subject to U.S. sanctions under several U.S. laws (see CRS Report RS20871, *Iran Sanctions*, by Kenneth Katzman). In March 2008, the U.S. Department of Justice sanctioned Future Bank, headquartered in Bahrain, because it is controlled and partially owned by Iran's Bank Melli. The sanctions, under Executive Order 13382 (anti-proliferation), prevent U.S. citizens from participating in

---

[55] Adam Entous and Matthew Rosenberg. "U.S. Says Iran Helps Crackdown in Syria." *Wall Street Journal*, April 14, 2011.

[56] For a list of possible sanctions that could be imposed, see CRS Report RS20871, *Iran Sanctions*, by Kenneth Katzman.

transactions with Future Bank and require the freezing of any U.S.-based bank assets. The bank remains in operation.

The Bahrain unrest has clouded the prospects for further energy cooperation between the two countries. A 2007 Ahmadinejad visit to Bahrain resulted in a preliminary agreement for Bahrain to buy 1.2 billion cubic feet per day (for 25 years) of Iranian gas via an undersea pipeline to be built. The deal would have involved a $4 billion investment by Bahrain to develop Phases 15 and 16 of Iran's South Pars gas field, which presumably would be the source of the gas that Bahrain would import. The March 2009 comments of Nateq Nuri, discussed above, led to the suspension of this deal, and there has been no movement on the arrangement since.

Post-Saddam Iraq

Bahrain's participation in OIF, discussed above, came despite domestic opposition in Bahrain to that war. Because of its limited income, Bahrain did not contribute funds to Iraq reconstruction, but it attended the "Expanded Neighbors of Iraq" regional conference process which last met in Kuwait on April 22, 2008. That process wound down in late 2008 as Iraq stabilized. On October 16, 2008, Bahrain's first post-Saddam ambassador to Iraq (Saleh Ali al-Maliki) presented his credentials in Baghdad, in line with King Hamad's pledge to President Bush in March 2008 to appoint an ambassador to Iraq. However, Bahrain-Iraq relations have become tense to the extent that Iraq's Shiite-dominated government and population is perceived as sympathetic to Bahrain's opposition. On March 9, 2012, Iraqi Shiites rallied in support of Bahrain's Shiites on the same day as Bahrain's opposition mounted a major demonstration. King Hamad did not attend the March 27-29 Arab League summit in Baghdad, and Bahrain sent a relatively low-level delegation, as did the other GCC states with the exception of Kuwait.

Qatar Territorial Disputes[57]

The United States cooperates closely with both Qatar and Bahrain, which is why the dispute between these two GCC states was closely watched by U.S. policymakers. The resolution of the dispute has partly removed these tensions as an issue for U.S. Gulf policy. The territorial disputes between Qatar and Bahrain have roots in the 18th century, when the ruling families of both countries controlled parts of the Arabian peninsula. Both sides agreed to take the dispute to the International Court of Justice (ICJ) in 1991 after clashes in 1986 in which Qatar landed military personnel on a man-made reef (Fasht al-Dibal) that was in dispute, and took some Bahrainis prisoner. The ICJ ruled on March 16, 2001 in favor of Bahrain on the central dispute over the Hawar Islands. It ruled in favor of Qatar on ownership of the Fasht al-Dibal reef and the town of Zubara on the Qatari mainland, where some members of the Al Khalifa family were long buried. Two smaller islands, Janan and Hadd Janan, were ruled not part of the Hawar Islands group and were also awarded to Qatar. Qatar expressed disappointment over the ruling but said it accepted it as binding, and the two have since cooperated on major regional issues. Saudi mediation of the issue in the 1986-1991 period proved fruitless.

---

[57] See The Estimate. Dossier: The Bahrain-Qatar Border Dispute: The World Court Decision, Part 1 and Part 2. March 23, 2001, and April 6, 2001.

Arab-Israeli Issues

On the Arab-Israeli dispute, Bahrain has not been as significant a mediator or broker as have its larger neighbors in the Gulf or broader Middle East. However, Bahrain has at times advanced ideas to move the Arab-Israeli peace process forward. In July 2009, Crown Prince Salman authored an op-ed calling on the Arab states to do more to communicate directly with the Israeli people on their ideas for peaceful resolution of the dispute.[58] In October 2009, Bahrain's foreign minister called for direct talks with Israel. Like most Arab states, Bahrain is supporting the efforts of Palestinian Authority President Mahmoud Abbas to obtain U.N. recognition for a State of Palestine, despite U.S. opposition to doing so prior to a Palestinian-Israeli peace settlement.

Earlier, Bahrain participated in the 1990-1996 multilateral Arab-Israeli talks, and it hosted a session on the environment (October 1994). Bahrain did not follow Oman and Qatar in exchanging trade offices with Israel. In September 1994, all GCC states ceased enforcing secondary and tertiary boycotts of Israel while retaining the ban on direct trade (primary boycott). In conjunction with the U.S.-Bahrain FTA, Bahrain dropped the primary boycott and closed boycott-related offices in Bahrain.

Still, the Arab-Israeli dispute always has the potential to become a political issue within Bahrain. In October 2009, the elected COR passed a bill making it a crime (punishable by up to five years in jail) for Bahrainis to travel to Israel or hold talks with Israelis. The bill, which did not become law, apparently was a reaction to a visit by Bahraini officials to Israel in July 2009. The visit was to obtain the release of five Bahrainis taken prisoner by Israel when it seized a ship bound with goods for Gaza, which is controlled by Hamas. In June 2010, Sunni and Shiite Islamists in Bahrain held a demonstration to denounce the Israeli seizure of a ship in a flotilla intended to run the Israeli blockade of the Hamas-run Gaza Strip.

Economic Issues

Like the other Gulf states, Bahrain was affected by the international financial crisis of 2008-2009, but perhaps to a lesser extent than the wealthier states of Kuwait, UAE, and Saudi Arabia. Bahrain did not experience the construction and real estate "bubble" to the degree that this occurred in, for example, UAE. It is also apparently being affected by the 2011 unrest; in May 2011 Moody's, a bond rating agency, downgraded the quality of Bahrain's bonds, thereby costing the government more to borrow funds.

Bahrain has little cushion to deal with economic downturns. It has the lowest oil and gas reserves of the Gulf monarchy states, estimated respectively at 210 million barrels of oil and 5.3 trillion cubic feet of gas. Some economic statistics are presented in **Table 3**. Without the ample oil or gas resources of its neighbors, Bahrain has diversified its economy by emphasizing banking and financial services (about 25.5% of GDP). At current rates of production (35,000 barrels per day of crude oil), Bahrain's onshore oil reserves will be exhausted in 15 years, but Saudi Arabia shares equally with Bahrain the 300,000 barrels per day produced from the offshore Abu Safa field. The United States buys virtually no oil from Bahrain; the major U.S. import from it is aluminum. Aluminum and other manufacturing sectors in Bahrain account for the existence in Bahrain of a vibrant middle and working class among its citizens. However, these classes are largely

---

[58] "Arabs Need to Talk to the Israelis." *The Washington Post*, July 16, 2009.

composed of Shiites, and this has made many Shiites envious of the "ownership class" of Sunni Muslims. On the other hand, many Shiites own businesses and have done well economically.

To encourage reform and signal U.S. appreciation, the United States and Bahrain signed an FTA on September 14, 2004. Implementing legislation was signed January 11, 2006 (P.L. 109-169). However, in light of the unrest, the AFL-CIO has urged the United States to void the FTA on the grounds that Bahrain is preventing free association of workers and abridging their rights.

In 2012, the United States exported $1.21 billion worth of goods to Bahrain, about the same amount as in 2011. The United States imported $700 million in goods from that country, substantially more than the $520 million worth of imports in 2011 and the $420 million worth of imports in 2010. In 2005, total bilateral trade was about $780 million, suggesting that trade has more than doubled since the U.S.-Bahrain FTA.

Table 3. Some Basic Facts About Bahrain

Population	About 1.25 million, of which about 1 million are citizens
Religions	81% Muslim, 9% Christian, 10% other
GDP (purchasing power parity)	$33.6 billion (2012)
Budget	$8.4 billion revenues, $8.7 billion expenditures (2012)
Inflation Rate	0.3% (2011)
Unemployment Rate	15%
GDP Real Growth Rate	3.9% in 2012
Size of Bahrain Defense Forces (BDF)	About 13,000, plus about 1,200 National Guard. Some personnel are expatriates, including other Arab and Pakistani.

Source: CIA, *The World Factbook.*

Table 4. U.S. Assistance to Bahrain

($ in millions)

	FY2003	04	05	06	07	08	09	10	11	12	13	14
FMF	90.0	24.6	18.9	15.6	15	3.968	8.0	19.0	15.46	10	10	10
IMET	0.448	0.60	0.65	0.65	0.616	0.622	.661	.670	.435	.554	.725	.725
NADR			1.49	2.76	.776	0.744	.500	1.10	1.5	.50	.45	.45
"Section 1206"				5.3	24.54	4.3	16.2					
ESF/Dem. and Gov.												3.0

Notes: IMET = International Military Education and Training Funds, used mainly to enhance BDF military professionalism and promote U.S. values. NADR = Non-Proliferation, Anti-Terrorism, De-Mining and Related Programs, used to sustain Bahrain's counterterrorism capabilities and interdict terrorists. Section 1206 are DOD funds used to train and equip Bahrain's special forces, its coastal surveillance and patrol capabilities, and to develop its counterterrorism assessment capabilities. (Named for a section of the FY2006 Defense Authorization Act, P.L. 109-163.). FY2014 amounts from State Dept. documents and H.R. 3547 (P.L. 113-76)

Figure 1. Bahrain

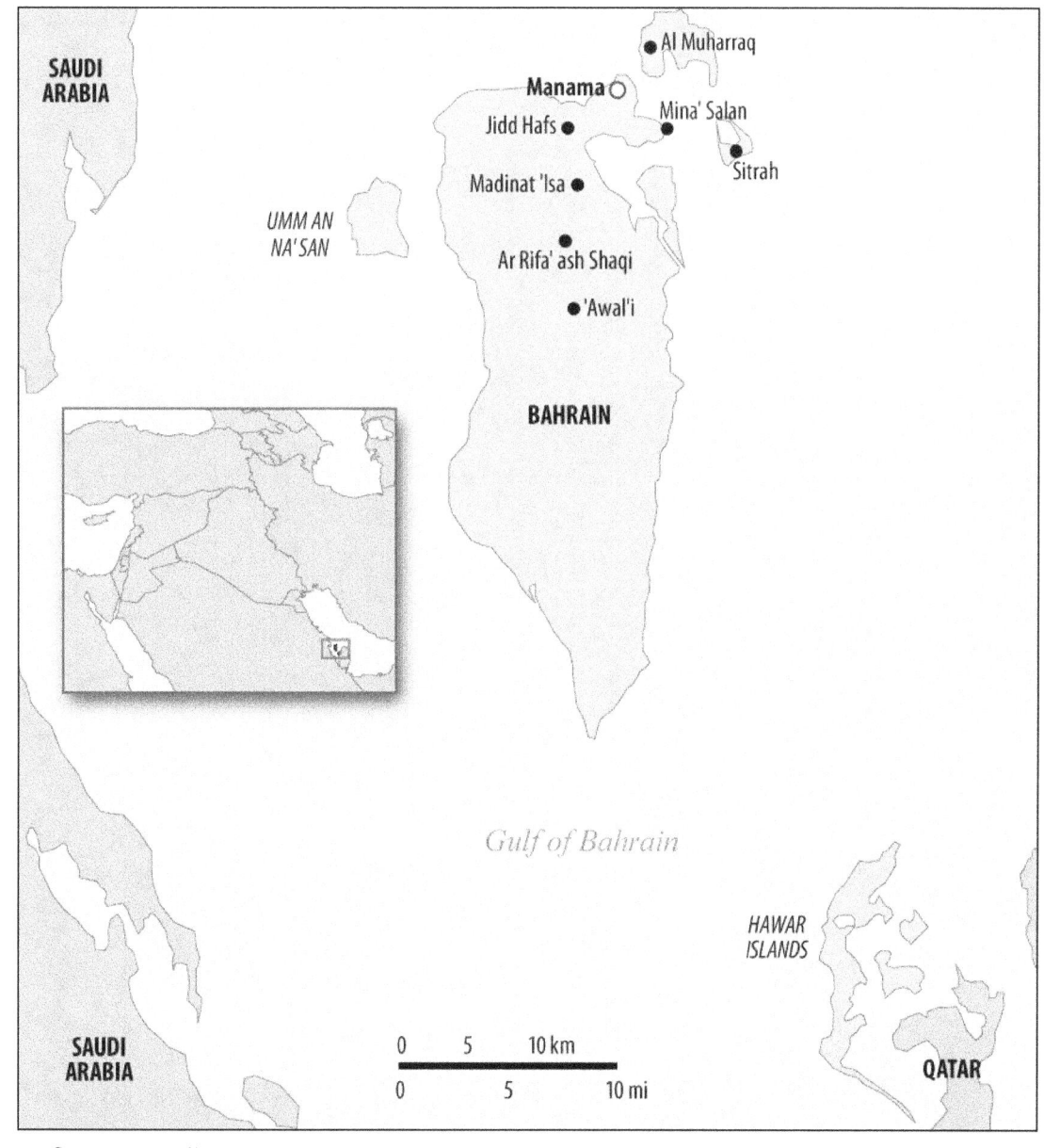

Source: https://www.cia.gov/library/publications/the-world-factbook/geos/ba.html.

Author Contact Information

Kenneth Katzman
Specialist in Middle Eastern Affairs
kkatzman@crs.loc.gov, 7-7612

www.ingramcontent.com/pod-product-compliance
Lightning Source LLC
Chambersburg PA
CBHW080635290526

45790CB00007B/3081